The Cognitive Semiotics of Film

In *The Cognitive Semiotics of Film*, Warren Buckland argues that the conflict between cognitive film theory and contemporary film theory is unproductive. Examining and developing the work of "cognitive film semiotics," a neglected branch of film theory that combines the insights of cognitive science with those of linguistics and semiotics, he investigates Michel Colin's cognitive semantic theory of film; Francesco Casetti's and Christian Metz's theories of film enunciation; Roger Odin's cognitive-pragmatic film theory; and Michel Colin's and Dominique Chateau's cognitive studies of film syntax, formulated within the framework of Noam Chomsky's transformational generative grammar. In presenting a survey of cognitive film semiotics, this study re-evaluates the film semiotics of the 1960s, highlights the weaknesses of American cognitive film theory, and challenges the move toward "post-theory" in film studies.

Warren Buckland is Lecturer in Screen Studies at Liverpool John Moores University. A former British Academy Post-doctoral Fellow, he is editor of *The Film Spectator: From Sign to Mind* and has contributed to *Screen*, *Semiotica*, and *Quarterly Review of Film and Video*.

The Cognitive Semiotics of Film

WARREN BUCKLAND

Liverpool John Moores University

CAMBRIDGE
UNIVERSITY PRESS

CAMBRIDGE UNIVERSITY PRESS
Cambridge, New York, Melbourne, Madrid, Cape Town, Singapore, São Paulo

Cambridge University Press
The Edinburgh Building, Cambridge CB2 8RU, UK

Published in the United States of America by Cambridge University Press, New York

www.cambridge.org
Information on this title: www.cambridge.org/9780521780056

First published 2000
This digitally printed version 2007

A catalogue record for this publication is available from the British Library

Library of Congress Cataloguing in Publication data
Buckland, Warren.
   The cognitive semiotics of film / Warren Buckland.
      p. cm.
   Includes bibliographical references and index.
   ISBN 0-521-78005-5
      1. Motion pictures – Semiotics.   I. Title.
   PN1995 .B796 2000
   791.43'01'4 – dc21
                                        00-026227

ISBN 978-0-521-78005-6 hardback
ISBN 978-0-521-03715-0 paperback

For Thomas Elsaesser

Contents

Preface and Acknowledgements

Two historians meet at a conference. The one asks the other: "What do you think are the main consequences of the French Revolution?" To which the other responds: "It is too early to tell." In this book I argue that it is still too early to tell what are the consequences of another revolution – the rise of the Language Analysis tradition, whose origins are to be found in the work of Saussure, Peirce, Wittgenstein, and so on, at the beginning of the twentieth century. As is well known, the Language Analysis tradition has already had a decisive impact on the formation and development of modern (or 'contemporary') film theory from the sixties onwards. One reason it is still too early to determine the consequences of the tradition is that the revolution it inaugurated is not complete. The main characteristic of this tradition is that it opposes the philosophy of consciousness, which dominated Western thought from the seventeenth century up to the work of the British idealists at the end of the nineteenth century. The Language Analysis tradition challenged the idealism inherent in the philosophy of the subject and replaced it with a new *mentalité* that reorients thinking toward language and other semiotic systems.

The conflict between the Language Analysis tradition and the philosophy of the subject can be understood today as a conflict between linguistics and cognitive science (or non-linguistic areas of cognitive science). Since the eighties, film theory has restaged this conflict, with the cognitive film theorists, such as David Bordwell, opposing the modern film theorists, such as Christian Metz, whose film theory is based on linguistics and semiotics.

This book begins from the premise that an outright conflict between cognitive film theory and modern film theory is unproductive and then moves on to consider in some detail a branch of modern film theory that combines the insights of cognitive science with linguistics and semiotics. In Chapter 1, I call these modern film theorists the 'cognitive film semioticians' and trace the influence of pragmatic theories of language, together with Noam Chomsky's linguistics, on their work. The result, as the rest of this book attempts to demonstrate, is a cognitive semiotics of film, which combines the insights of both cognitive film theory and modern film theory.

This book not only presents a survey of the cognitive film semiotics written from the mid-seventies up to the present time, but also offers a brief survey of American cognitive film theory and traces modern film theory's foundations back to the Language Analysis tradition. In the following pages I therefore argue that modern film theory constitutes one of the disciplines of that tradition and that it has a future since it has shifted its level of analysis – from (in Noam Chomsky's terms) the level of observational adequacy (the segmentation and classification of a corpus of texts into its ultimate paradigmatic constituents) to the level of descriptive adequacy (the analysis of the rules and institutions that generate texts, rules, and institutions that are defined in cognitive terms).

The analysis is framed by Charles Morris's well known distinction between syntax, semantics, and pragmatics. Chapter 2 studies the cognitive semantic theory of film developed by Michel Colin. Chapter 3 investigates recent theorizing into the enunciative dimension of film (a narrow pragmatic theory), as carried out by Francesco Casetti and Christian Metz; Chapter 4 outlines the continuing work of Roger Odin into a broad, cognitive-pragmatic theory of film. Finally, Chapter 5 sets out the results of recent studies, by Michel Colin and Dominique Chateau, into the grammar (or syntax) of film, which they carried out within the framework of Chomsky's transformational generative grammar.

The relation between this book and the semiotics of Charles Morris ends on this terminological borrowing. Morris's semiotics is behaviorist, whereas the film theory surveyed in this study attempts to combine semiotics with cognitive science. The ultimate aim of this study is to chart the interface between the Language Analysis tradition and cognitive science as articulated in the work of the cognitive film semioticians.

A significantly different version of Chapter 5 has been published under the title "Michel Colin and the Psychological Reality of Film

Semiology," *Semiotica*, 107, 1/2 (1995): 51–79. Sections of the other chapters have been presented at the following conferences and symposia: Hommage à Christian Metz (University of Amsterdam, March 25, 1994); Fifth Congress of the International Association for Semiotic Studies (University of California, Berkeley, June 12–18, 1994); Semiotics of the Media (University of Kassel, Germany, March 20–23, 1995); Post-doctoral Fellowship Symposium (The British Academy, London, December 8, 1995); and the Society of Cinema Studies Conference (Dallas, Texas, March 7–10, 1996).

Finally, I would like to thank all those who have read various chapters and have offered suggestions for revision, as well as those who have provided general guidance and support: Richard Allen, Edward Branigan, Robert Burgoyne, Glen Creeber, Kevin Donnelly, Alison McMahan, Winfried Nöth, Roger Odin, Karen Pehla, Jan Simons, Murray Smith, and Michael Wedel. I owe a special thanks to Thomas Elsaesser for encouraging me over the last twelve years to persevere in the face of adversity. His intellectual strength has enabled me to overcome many of my intellectual weaknesses.

This work was funded by a British Academy Post-doctoral Fellowship, which I held at the University of East Anglia (UEA). I wish to thank my former colleagues at UEA (Charles Barr, Pam Cook, and Andrew Higson) for creating a suitable environment in which to conduct this research, and the British Academy for its generous financial support as well as for its recognition of film studies as a legitimate subject to fund at post-doctoral level.

This book is accompanied by my anthology *The Film Spectator: From Sign to Mind* (Amsterdam: Amsterdam University Press, 1995), which collects for the first time in English the work of the cognitive film semioticians discussed in the following chapters.

CHAPTER ONE

The Cognitive Turn in Film Theory

> We have witnessed a number of attempts to by-pass [film theory's] most difficult conceptual problems by replacing it with something else. The "something else" is sometimes film history or aesthetics; sometimes it is a new object, such as television, popular culture, video; and sometimes it is a question of new methodologies, which may resemble dusted off methodologies from the social sciences, such as audience questionnaires or interviews, procedures that haven't benefitted from the literature in the social sciences that has interrogated its own methods and limitations. (Janet Bergstrom)[1]

During the eighties, film studies gradually adopted 'new' methodologies from cultural studies and the social sciences, which displaced the speculative ideas of film theory. Rather than construct hypotheses and models about the general structure and spectators' experience of film, film studies has moved toward the 'something else' enumerated by Janet Bergstrom. However, a number of film scholars, in both Europe and North America, have persisted with film theory's most difficult conceptual problems, which they tackle from the perspective of cognitive science. This book is a report on the knowledge generated by these cognitive film theorists. But because this knowledge is fragmentary and incomplete, I have endeavored to expand and develop it in new and unforeseen ways.

However, for the most part, I do not report on the knowledge generated by the well-known cognitive film theorists in North America (David Bordwell, Noël Carroll, Edward Branigan, Joseph Anderson, among others) but discuss the much lesser known film theorists working in the cognitive tradition in Europe – particularly Francesco Casetti, Roger Odin, Michel Colin, and Dominique Chateau.[2]

Despite their similarities, the two groups evidence a marked

1

contrast in their work: Whereas the North American cognitivists decisively reject the basic doctrines of modern film theory (a.k.a. 'contemporary' film theory, based upon structural linguistics, semiotics, Marxism, and psychoanalysis), the European cognitivists inaugurate a revolution in modern film theory by returning to and transforming its early stage – that is, the semiotic stage.[3] Both groups therefore reject psychoanalysis and replace it with cognitive science. However, the European cognitivists assimilate cognitive science into a semiotic framework, whereas the North American cognitivists work within a pure cognitive framework (one untainted by semiotics).

Treating the work of a group of individuals as representing a homogeneous position is always risky. Nonetheless, all the North American cognitivists I have named belong to the Institute for Cognitive Studies in Film and Video, which to some extent unifies the agenda of the individual authors.[4] What unifies the European cognitivists is that their work critically responds to Christian Metz's film semiotics. This response involves transforming Metz's semiotics by means of theories of pragmatics, cognitive science, and transformational generative grammar (which is in fact one of the main research programs in cognitive science). The European cognitivists attempt to overcome the 'translinguistics' of Metz's film semiotics – that is, Metz's insistence that film semiotics be based exclusively on the methods of structural linguistics – by combining semiotics with pragmatics and cognitive science. Structural linguists over-emphasize language's rigid, limiting capacity, and a semiotics based exclusively on structural linguistics conceptualizes all other semiotic systems in a similarly rigid manner – limiting and conditioning the meaning of human experience – at the expense of the language user's reflective and creative capacities to manipulate signs. By combining semiotics with cognitive science, the European cognitivists restore the balance and begin to conceptualize natural language and other semiotic systems as both enabling and limiting. Because of the dual emphasis in the work of the European cognitivists on semiotics and cognitive science, I shall call them the 'cognitive film semioticians'.[5] Figure 1 shows the relations among the classical film theory of the 1930s–1950s, modern film theory, the North American cognitivists (from now on, simply 'the cognitivists'), and the cognitive film semioticians.

In this book I aim to outline the common theoretical assump-

1. CLASSICAL FILM THEORY
   (a) Montagists (Rudolf Arnheim, Sergei Eisenstein, etc.)
   (b) Realists (André Bazin, Siegfried Kracauer, etc.)
2. MODERN FILM THEORY (a.k.a. 'contemporary' film theory)
   (a) Film semiotics (Christian Metz of *Film Language, Language and Cinema*)
   (b) Post-structural film theory (a.k.a. second semiotics, psycho-semiotics): Marxist and psychoanalytic film theory of Stephen Heath, Colin MacCabe, Metz of *The Imaginary Signifier*, Jean-Louis Comolli, Jean-Louis Baudry, Raymond Bellour, etc. (the transition from 2a to 2b was effected by theories of enunciation based on the linguistics of Benveniste)
3. COGNITIVE FILM THEORY
   David Bordwell, Noël Carroll, Edward Branigan, Joseph Anderson, Torben Grodal, Ed Tan, Murray Smith
4. COGNITIVE FILM SEMIOTICS (development from 2a)
   (a) New theories of enunciation (Francesco Casetti, Metz of *The Impersonal Enunciation*)
   (b) Semio-pragmatics of film (Roger Odin)
   (c) Transformational generative grammar and cognitive semantics of film (Michel Colin, Dominique Chateau)

Fig. 1

tions held by cognitive film semioticians and clarify their relation to the broader traditions of twentieth century intellectual thought. Cognitive film semiotics represents the next stage – and arguably the maturation of – semiotic film theory. Despite the revolution it has inaugurated, cognitive film semiotics remains virtually unknown in Anglo-American film studies. This is unfortunate because it develops a more informed understanding – than either semiotics or cognitive science alone – of film's underlying structure, together with the way spectators comprehend films. By writing this book I hope to introduce cognitive film semiotics to the Anglo-American community of film scholars and, more generally, encourage a re-evaluation of the role of semiotics in film theory.

Before outlining cognitive film semiotics, I shall briefly review the cognitivists' position, particularly their reasons for rejecting linguistics and semiotics as viable paradigms for studying film. I shall also attempt to point out several problems with their purely cognitive-based film theory.

To what extent is the dispute between modern film theory and cognitivism based on conceptual disagreement, and to what extent is it simply based on misunderstanding? Briefly, I shall argue that the cognitivists' criticism of the psychoanalytic dimension of modern film theory is based on conceptual disagreement and, moreover, that this disagreement is partly justified. However, I shall also argue that the cognitivists' critique of the linguistic and semiotic dimensions of modern film theory is based on misunderstanding, which has led them to refute its premises falsely.

If film theory is to make any advances, it needs to establish the grounds for disagreement among its various schools and must identify misunderstandings. Peter Lehman argues that scholars should develop a dialogue with other scholars. He asks: "How do we teach students to respectfully argue with the perspectives of their peers or teachers if the materials that they read encourage them to dismiss those critical methodologies and film styles with which they are not in agreement?" And: "Students should also realize that what they can learn from someone may have little or nothing to do with their agreement with that person's methodology or critical judgement."[6] Similarly, Noël Carroll argues that "film theorizing should be dialectical," adding: "By that I mean that a major way in which film theorizing progresses is by criticizing already existing theory. Some may say that my use of the term 'progresses' here is itself suspect. However, I count the elimination of error as progress and that is one potential consequence, it is to be hoped, of dialectical criticism. Of course, an even more salutary consequence might be that in criticizing one theoretical solution to a problem, one may also see one's way to a better solution."[7] Carroll's recent position is to develop a dialogue with, rather than simply condemn, previous theories of film.

In the following review of cognitivism, I do not aim to be dismissive, but to be critical. This involves clarifying misunderstandings so that we can leave behind us the old disagreements and make advancements by tackling new disagreements.

The cognitivists find very little of value or interest in modern film theory, although in *Narration in the Fiction Film* Bordwell acknowledges the value of some early semiotic work, such as Christian Metz's *grande syntagmatique*.[8] Yet Bordwell undermines this acknowledgement in Chapter 2 of the same book when he asks the following questions:

Why . . . is the employment of linguistic concepts a necessary condition of analyzing filmic narration? Is linguistics presumed to offer a way of subsuming film under a general theory of signification? Or does linguistics offer methods of inquiry which we can adopt? Or is linguistics simply a storehouse of localized and suggestive analogies to cinematic processes?[9]

I shall take each question in turn. Moreover, I shall use my responses as an opportunity to review the previous research carried out in the name of film semiotics.

1. *"Why . . . is the employment of linguistic concepts a necessary condition of analyzing filmic narration?"*

The simple answer is that the employment of linguistics is *not* necessary to the analysis of filmic narration. Bordwell is right to criticize Metz's translinguistic standpoint. Metz initially made the mistake of arguing that linguistics is a necessary condition for analyzing filmic narration because he equated film language with narrativity: *"It is precisely to the extent that the cinema confronted the problems of narration that . . .* it came to produce a body of specific signifying procedures."[10] However, he challenged this equation in *Language and Cinema,*[11] a book that marks the maturation of his semiotic thinking on film. Perhaps we could turn this question back to Bordwell and ask, Why is his historical poetics of cinema predominately a poetics of narration?[12]

2. *"Is linguistics presumed to offer a way of subsuming film under a general theory of signification?"*

The short answer to whether linguistics subsumes film under a general theory of signification is yes. To think of film within a general theory of signification has many consequences, several of which I shall outline.

Film semiotics is a project that does not consider 'film' to be an unproblematic, pregiven entity, but reflects on the very nature of film's existence, together with the consequences it has on culture and society. Semioticians challenge the commonsense ideological understanding of film as a mere form of harmless entertainment, maintaining that it is a system of signification that articulates experience. This is a relevant framework in which to examine film because the more complex a society becomes, the more it relies upon systems of signification to structure, simplify, and organize experience. The fundamental premise of semiotics is that "the whole of human experience, without exception, is an interpretive structure mediated and sustained by signs."[13] Semiotics offers an all-embracing theory of human culture – or, more precisely, of human experience, belief, and knowledge. It is a theory in which humans are posited to have an indirect – mediated – relation to their environment. I will argue that natural language plays a decisive role in this process of mediation, of enabling individuals to control and understand their environment. But natural language is not all-encompassing, for human culture consists of numerous other semiotic systems – such as film – that also mediate between individuals and their environment. Perhaps it is relevant here to note that my discussion is limited to anthroposemiotics (the study of human signs) and does not cover zoosemiotics (the study of animal communication), although both are united under biosemiotics (the study of communication generated by all living organisms). Linguistics, the study of natural language, is one of the dominant branches of anthroposemiotics but has a very small role to play in biosemiotics and is not involved in zoosemiotics.

Studying film from a semiotic perspective does not involve comparing it to natural language (although this is one of the secondary consequences of conducting a semiotic analysis of film), but involves first and foremost analyzing film's specificity. In film semiotics, specificity is defined in terms of the invariant traits manifest in all films, the traits that confer upon film its distinctiveness, which determines its unique means of articulating and mediating experience. Film semioticians define specificity not in terms of film's invariant surface (immediately perceptible) traits, but of its underlying (non-perceptible and non-manifest) system of invariant traits. This semiotic perspective opposes the work of the classical film theorists, who also studied filmic specificity. However, they defined specificity in terms of film's immediately perceptible traits, a focus that resulted in their formulating two mutually contradictory theories of filmic specificity. Rudolf Arnheim argued that filmic specificity lies in unique 'distorting' properties (especially montage) that demonstrate film's specific representation of perceptual reality – its presentation of a unique perspective on reality. However, André Bazin argued that its specificity lies in the ability – for the first time in the history of art – to record 'reality' without the intervention of the human hand (that is, he argued that film's specificity lies in its existential link to reality). He advocated that filmmakers not subsume film's ability to record under distortive techniques such as montage. Instead, he advocated a style of filmmaking to exploit the recording capacity of film – such as the long take, deep focus, and camera movement – which maintains the film's existential link to reality. Metz sought to surmount these two mutually contradictory theories by defining specificity in terms of film's underlying system of invariant traits. To present an understanding of what 'underlying system of invariant traits' means and how it enabled Metz to surmount the contradictions of classical film theory, I need to give an overview of semiotics.

Semiotics is premised on the hypothesis that all types of phenomena have a corresponding underlying system that constitutes both the specificity and intelligibility of those phenomena. The role of theory in semiotics is to make visible the underlying, non-perceptible system by constructing a model of it. A model "is an independent object which stands in a certain correspondence with (not identical with, and not completely different from) the object of cognition and which, being a mediating link in cognition, can replace the object of cognition in certain relations and give the researcher a certain amount of information, which is transferred by certain rules of correspondence on the object of modelling. The need for a model arises when for some reason immediate analysis of an object is inexpedient or impossible."[14]

The first step in developing a semiotic film theory is to construct a model of the non-perceptible system underlying films, which involves identifying the properties and parts of this underlying system, together with the way they interrelate and function. The resulting model is expressed in a series of hypotheses, or speculative propositions. These propositions are not obviously true or false but are probable. The validity of these probable propositions and the models they construct is dependent on both internal and external criteria. Internally, hypotheses and models must display logical consistency. Externally, they must be able to analyze existing phenomena and 'predict' the structure of new phenomena. Semiotic film theory can be validated or invalidated on the basis of its logical (in)consistency, as well as its (in)ability to attribute structure to a given or new film – which involves relating the film to the semiotician's prior model of the underlying system. In other words, external validity is dependent upon the model's possession of generality – its ability to be applied to all phenomena, given and new.

Metz attempted to construct a general model of the system underlying all films. His first model, to be discussed, is the *grande syntagmatique;* his second, developed in *Language and Cinema,* attempts to define filmic specificity in terms of a specific combination of five overlapping traits – iconicity, mechanical duplication, multiplicity, movement, and mechanically produced multiple moving images.[15] Taken individually, Metz realized, none of these traits is specific to the cinema; the specificity of cinema, he argues, lies in their specific combination. These five traits are not simply heaped together but are organized into a particular system, which Metz models in terms of overlapping circles, similar to a Venn diagram (although Metz does not go so far as to visualize this model; this is what I have done in Figure 2). Filmic specificity for Metz consists of the five traits and of the system that organizes them. Notice that Metz does not draw any direct comparisons between film and natural language in this semiotic model of film. Although it is possible to question the logical consistency of Metz's mode of reasoning in *Language and Cinema,* my aim in discussing this book is simply to outline the semiotic model Metz developed there. The primary problem with this model is its generalizability, because it leaves out some avant-garde films that do not employ mechanical duplication (for example, the films of Len Lye) and films that do not employ movement (the most celebrated example is Chris Marker's *La Jetée*).

Like other semiotic studies, film semiotics adopts the two tier hierarchy between perceptible and non-perceptible levels of reality and formulates probable hypotheses describing this underlying, non-perceptible level. The ultimate objective of film semiotics is to construct a model of the non-perceptible system underlying all films. Whereas Saussure called the specific underlying system of natural languages *la langue,* in opposition to the surface phenomena, *la parole,* Noam Chomsky calls the underlying system competence, in opposition to performance, and for Metz, the specific underlying system of film is called cinematic language, in opposition to individual films.

The function of a model is therefore to mediate between a theory and its object of study. Semioticians do not commit the fallacy of identifying the real object with the object of knowledge because

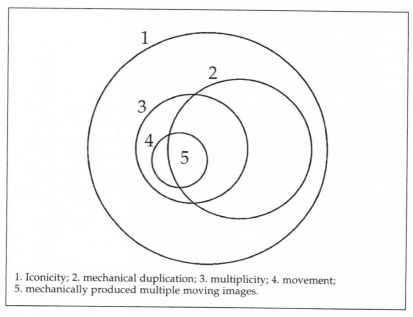

1. Iconicity; 2. mechanical duplication; 3. multiplicity; 4. movement;
5. mechanically produced multiple moving images.

Fig. 2

they realize that each theoretical framework does not *discover* its specific object of study but must *construct* it, precisely because the object of study is inaccessible to perception. Saussure realized this in relation to the specific object of semiotic study: "The object is not given in advance of the viewpoint: far from it. Rather, one might say that it is the viewpoint adopted which creates [*crée*] the object."[16] For Samuel Weber, "This assertion marks out the epistemological space of Saussure's theoretical effort, and to neglect its far-reaching implications has inevitably meant to misconstrue the status of his arguments."[17] In order not to misconstrue Saussure's arguments, I need to point out that semiotics *constructs* a model of its object of study; it does not *create* its object of study (despite Saussure's use of the verb *créer* in the preceding quotation).

To answer adequately Bordwell's second question – "Is linguistics presumed to offer a way of subsuming film under a general theory of signification?" – we need to go further into semiotic theory. The underlying system is "an imperceptible content lending structure to the perceptible insofar as it signifies and conveys precisely the historical experience of the individual and group."[18] Semioticians call this non-perceptible, underlying system, which lends structure to the perceptible, a system of codes. One of the integral (although by no means encompassing) codes of human culture is natural language. It is a species-specific system that distinguishes humans from animals and that humans use to develop a shared understanding of the world.

A system of codes consists of the prior set of finite, invariant traits of a language, together with their rules for combination. Speech (*la parole*) is generated by two processes: Codes are selected from the underlying system, and they are combined according to rules. Both processes constitute the intelligibility of speech because meaning is the product of the structural relations that exist between the codes. Speech can then be analyzed in terms of the underlying system of codes that generated it.[19] In semiotics, 'code' is therefore a term that designates the underlying system that constitutes the specificity of, lends structure to, and confers intelligibility on phenomena.

In analyzing film from a semiotic perspective, film scholars bring to film theory a new level of filmic reality. They successfully demonstrate that the impression of unity and continuity each spectator experiences at the cinema is based on a shared, non-perceptible underlying system of codes that constitutes the specificity of, lends structure to, and confers intelligibility on the perceptible level of film. Early film semioticians applied the structural linguistic methodology of segmentation and classification to identify the non-perceptible system underlying a film. The setting up of this hierarchy – between the perceptible level of film and the non-perceptible system of codes underlying it – is the main contribution semioticians have so far made to film theory. They show that filmic continuity is a surface illusion, what Marxist critics call the 'impression of reality'. In effect, semiotics enables film theorists to drive a wedge between film and its referent, to break the supposedly existential link between them, and to demonstrate that filmic meaning is a result of a system of codes, not the relation between images and referents.

Once film semioticians identified the hierarchy between the perceptible and the non-perceptible, what were their main 'objects' of study? Very simply, they began to construct models of the various underlying systems that determine the surface – perceptible – level of film. It is at this point that film semioticians moved away from analyzing cinematic language (or filmic specificity) and created a theory of textual analysis, motivating the study of underlying systems that determine the textual structure of the particular film under discussion, including the cause-effect narrative logic, the process of narrativization, the spatio-temporal relations between shots, the patterns of repetition and difference, and specific filmic techniques such as the eyeline match.

The identification and analysis of all these underlying systems are a result of subsuming film under a general theory of signification. Bordwell may protest that the Russian Formalists studied many of these filmic mechanisms, but, as is well known, Saussure's structural linguistics directly influenced the Russian Formalists.

3. *"Does linguistics offer methods of inquiry which we can adopt?"*

Linguistics does offer methods of inquiry that film theorists can adopt. I shall refer to the most obvious example: Early film semioticians borrowed from structural linguistics the commutation test, a deductive method of analyzing how the underlying level lends structure to the surface level. This method consists of the activities of segmentation and classification. In principle, a commutation involves the correlation between a change on the surface level and a change on the underlying level. A change on the surface may be either a variation of the same code or a new code. By means of the commutation test, semioticians can identify the changes on the surface level that correlate with the changes on the underlying level.

The commutation test enabled Saussure to describe speech (*la parole*) as an infinity of messages generated by a finite, underlying system (*la langue*). The concept of 'identity' enabled him to reduce the infinity of speech to this finite system, for he recognized that all speech is composed from the same small number of invariant codes used recursively in different combinations. Saussure did not conceive of this system as a mere conglomerate of codes, but as a series of interdependent, formal relationships. Furthermore – and here Saussure located the 'ultimate law of language' – he defined codes only in terms of their relation, or *difference*, to other codes (both the paradigmatic relations they enter into in the underlying system and the syntagmatic relations they enter into in speech).

The theory of commutation, based on the analytic methods of segmentation and classification, led Metz (in his essay "Problems of Denotation in the Fiction Film") to formulate the *grande syntagmatique* that Bordwell praised in the Preface to *Narration in the*

Fiction Film. For Metz the *grande syntagmatique* designates one of the primary codes underlying and lending structure to all classical films. It represents a prior set of finite sequence (or syntagmatic) types, a paradigm of syntagms from which a filmmaker can choose to represent profilmic events in a particular sequence. Metz defines each syntagma according to the spatio-temporal relations that exist between the profilmic events it depicts. Syntagmas are commutable because the same events depicted by means of a different syntagma will have a different meaning.[20] Metz detected eight different types of syntagma in total, each of which is identifiable by a specific spatio-temporal relationship existing between its images. These syntagmas form a finite paradigm of invariant codes to the extent that they offer eight different commutable ways of constructing an image sequence. The eight syntagmatic types therefore conform to Saussure's 'ultimate law of language', because each syntagma is defined in terms of its relation, or difference, to the other syntagmas. For Metz: "These montage figures [film syntagmas] derive their meaning to a large extent in relation to one another. One, then, has to deal, so to speak, with a paradigm of syntagmas. It is only by a sort of *commutation* that one can identify and enumerate them."[21] Notice again that this semiotic model does not draw any direct comparisons between film and natural language.

4. *"Is linguistics simply a storehouse of localized and suggestive analogies to cinematic processes?"*

This final question, more rhetorical than the others, reveals Bordwell's preferred way of characterizing modern film theory. Ideally, my responses to the previous three questions have shown that linguistics offers film theorists more than a storehouse of localized and suggestive analogies. Moreover, linguistics does not encourage the majority of film semioticians to draw analogies between film and natural language. Metz adopted a scholastic method of theorizing, in which he considered all the arguments that can be advanced for or against an hypothesis – in this instance, the comparison between film language and natural language – to determine its degree of credibility. The bulk of his first essay "Cinéma: langue ou langage?" advances arguments *against* the temptation to draw analogies between film language and natural language.[22] Metz realized that the two languages belong to different logical categories, and that recognition led him to conclude that film is a *"langage sans langue.''*[23] In his later work, Metz went on to carry out the primary aim of film semiotics – to construct a model of filmic specificity, film's underlying system. In constructing the *grande syntagmatique* he confused filmic specificity with narrativity, but later, in *Language and Cinema*, he defined specificity in terms of a specific combination of five traits, plus the underlying system that organizes them.

To summarize my responses to Bordwell's four questions, the very idea of 'cinematic language' for film semioticians is not simply an analogy (as it was in the prelinguistic film-language comparisons of Raymond Spottiswoode, the filmology movement, etc.); that is, the semioticians' analysis of film is not premised on identifying any direct resemblance between film and natural language. Instead, film semioticians argue that film is a medium that possesses its own distinctive, underlying system that confers intelligibility on and lends structure to all films. Of course, semioticians do not pretend to study everything that makes a film intelligible; instead, they limit their analysis to the invariant traits that define film's specificity.

What about the cognitivists' critique of other domains of modern film theory? One of the dominant reasons the cognitivists criticize modern film theory is the behaviorism implicit in its account of subject positioning, in which the spectator is automatically and unfailingly positioned as an ideological subject, with no cognitive capacity to process and manipulate the film. In other words, the modern film theorists posited a direct, unmediated relation between the stimulus and the spectator's response, which, as Bordwell observes, "impute[s] a fundamental passivity to the spectator."[24] This criticism is certainly valid and justifies the need for a cognitive account of the spectator's processing activity. But does it also justify rejecting semiotics? The argument I develop is that a cognitive theory of film that assimilates semiotics overcomes the problems of translinguistics, the behaviorism of modern film theory's account of subject positioning, together with the cognitivists' overemphasis on the spectator as an autonomous rational self. The cognitivists, on the other hand, argue that film theorists need to reject semiotics and start again by developing a cognitive theory of spectatorship untainted by semiotics. Bordwell and others ask, Why does a cognitive theory of film need to refer to language and semiotics? My immediate answer is that we need to consider the specificity of the human mind and culture. Whereas the Enlightenment

philosophers argued that reasoning is specific to humanity, twentieth century philosophers belonging to the Language Analysis tradition, together with semioticians, realize that language is specific
to humanity. Language is not just another aspect of the human
mind, but is its defining characteristic. I shall have more to say on
the Language Analysis tradition later.

In opposition to modern film theory, Bordwell argues that "a
film . . . does not 'position' anybody. A film cues the spectator to
execute a definable variety of *operations*."[25] Bordwell then proceeds
to fill in the mental blanks left by the behaviorist stance of modern
film theory. But by arguing that a film does not position anybody,
Bordwell suggests that the spectator is a context-free 'entity' and
that film viewing is a purely rationalist activity. I agree with Bordwell that spectators are not positioned or placed by a film in the
narrow sense of the modern film theorists (as Bordwell writes, the
terms 'position' and 'place' "lead us to conceive of the perceiver as
backed into a corner by conventions of perspective, editing, narrative point of view, and psychic unity."[26]) We can reject this narrow
conception of spectatorship without rejecting the proposition that a
film modifies the spectator's mind in a specific way.[27]

To varying degrees cognitivists downplay or reject the anthro-
posemiotic dimension of filmic comprehension and instead focus
on its ecological dimension. The following cognitivists are key to
the ecological approach: Joseph Anderson, the Australian philoso-
pher Gregory Currie, the Danish film theorist Torben Grodal, and
the Dutch film theorist Ed Tan.[28] Edward Branigan and David
Bordwell also develop ecological theories, but to a lesser extent.
(Since its initial development in North America, cognitive film theory has therefore become international and has developed an ecological framework at the same time.) The flavour of this work can
be summed up in the following extract from Grodal's *Moving Pictures*:

Visual fiction is viewed in a conscious state, and is mostly about human
beings perceiving, acting, and feeling in, or in relation to, a visible and
audible world. The viewer's experience and the phenomena experienced
often demand explanations that imply non-conscious activities; but the
emotions and cognitions must be explained in relation to conscious mental
states and processes. For evolutionary reasons, it is improbable that the
way phenomena appear in consciousness is just an illusion caused by
certain quite different non-conscious agents and mechanisms.[29]

By ignoring each other, cognitivists and semioticians have developed unbalanced theories of the cinema. In our search to understand how films are understood, we need to maintain a balance between cultural constraints, such as language and other semiotic systems of human culture, and broader ecological constraints. The cognitive film semioticians go some way to achieving this balance, in opposition to the linguistic determinism of Metz's film semiotics and the free will and rational autonomy the cognitivists confer upon film spectators. Each of the following chapters charts the way the cognitive film semioticians attempt to maintain this balance, although there is variation among them.

The Language Analysis Tradition

The Language Analysis tradition incorporates the analytic philosophy of Frege, Carnap, Moore, Russell, Ryle, and Wittgenstein; the structural linguistics of Saussure; the pragmatics of Habermas; and the semiotics of C. S. Peirce. Its primary aim is to transform questions about epistemology and the mind into questions about language and meaning. Karl-Otto Apel defines the Language Analysis tradition as (following Aristotle) a *prima philosophia*: "First Philosophy was founded by the Greeks as an *ontology* of the essential structure of things; . . . later on, in the so-called 'new age', it was transformed into, or replaced by, a *critical epistemology* . . . ; and . . . finally, in the 20th century, both ontology and epistemology were questioned or transformed by *language analysis*."[30]

The three hundred year domination of epistemology, or the philosophy of the subject, in Western philosophy began with Descartes, reached its peak in the subjective idealism of Kant and Fichte, and was completed in the objective idealism of Hegel and the British idealists (Bosanquet and Bradley). The significance of the transformation from the idealism of epistemology to Language Analysis was that language, signs, and the process of semiosis replaced mental entities. For example, semiotics and structuralism initiated a radical critique of Kant's subjective idealism without attacking reason and rationality (which led Paul Ricoeur to call structuralism "Kantianism without the transcendental subject"). Semioticians relocated reason and rationality in language and sign systems, rather than in the mind. For Jürgen Habermas, "The structuralist approach follows Saussure's lead and begins with the model provided by grammatical rule systems; and it overcomes the philosophy of the subject when it traces the achievements of the knowing and acting subject, who is bound up in his linguistic practices, back to the foundational structures and generative rules of a grammar. Subjectivity thereby loses the power of spontaneously generating a world."[31] Within analytic philosophy, Gilbert Ryle wrote a devastating critique of Cartesian dualism in *The Concept of Mind*.[32] More generally, analytic philosophers privileged language by conceiving of philosophical problems as mere confusions and misunderstandings over language use, rather than as conflicts or disagreements over substantive issues. Analytic philosophy therefore set itself up as a therapeutic activity that aims to dissolve philosophical problems by clarifying the meaning of words and expressions. Meanwhile, Frege replaced psychologism with logical analysis, and C. S. Peirce transformed Descartes's method of introspection and Kantian epistemology into semiotics.[33]

Jürgen Habermas is well known for his attempts to continue the project of modernity, and the Enlightenment project from which it emerged. But he recognizes the limitations and failures of the Enlightenment project – most notably, its idealism. One dimension of Habermas's work consists of rereading the Enlightenment project from the perspective of linguistics – or, more accurately, the pragmatic theory of speech acts.[34] This enables him to update and transform the Enlightenment by replacing its idealism with Language Analysis, effecting a shift from the purely subjective to the intersubjective – language, dialogue, and communicative reason. His argument is that language is not simply one of many human possessions in the world; instead, it is the primary possession, since it constitutes the basis of humanity's understanding of the world and orients the individual into a shared interpretation of both the world and human actions. Habermas does not fall into a translinguistic trap because he is from the start focusing on human reasoning capacities. And he is not concerned with the "purism of pure reason," but with the way reason is concretized in language. The problem with the philosophy of the subject for Habermas is that it reifies subjectivity by conferring upon the individual a "narcissistically overinflated autonomy" because it overemphasizes "purposively rational self-assertion."[35] By contrast, Habermas – and the Language Analysis tradition generally – decentres subjectivity by arguing that it is not master of its own house, but is dependent on something that is a priori and intersubjective – language. And language is fundamental because it functions to represent (or disclose) reality, establishes interpersonal relations, and guides personal expression. In other words, it facilitates mutual understanding and coordinates social action: "Agreement arrived at through communication, which is measured by the intersubjective recognition of validity claims, makes possible a networking of social interactions and lifeworld contexts . . . The stratification of discourse and action built into communicative action takes the place of . . . prelinguistic and isolated reflection."[36] Habermas presents a strong case for replacing the idealism of the philosophy of the subject with Language Analysis. I shall develop this point in more detail in Chapter 2, when reviewing David Bordwell's cognitive theory of the spectator.

Language Analysis in all its forms therefore rejects idealism and mentalism, transforming the 'first person' perspective of epistemology (Descartes's method of introspection) to the 'third person' perspective of language and signs. Thomas Daddesio clearly sums up the issues involved:

The critique of introspection initiated by Peirce gained momentum when, with the rise of behaviorism in the social sciences, introspection was abandoned as a reputable method because it was perceived as being unable to provide the objective, repeatable observations that science requires. As long as it seemed reasonable – a circumstance that lasted roughly three hundred years – to believe that one could have privileged access to the contents of one's own mind, mental processes could be taken as foundational for both epistemology and accounts of human behavior. However, once this privilege came to be viewed as illusory, introspection was replaced by methods relying on a third-person perspective. From this new perspective, the access that individuals have to their own thoughts could no longer be taken as a foundation for knowledge and, consequently, private events were replaced, in discussions of language, meaning, and reason, by events that were open to public scrutiny such as the behavior of others, the words they utter, and the uses to which they put words.[37]

The epistemologists' assumptions of immediate access to the thoughts in one's own mind and the power of the mind to disclose reality were replaced by the Language Analysts' assumptions of indirect access to one's thoughts via language and other intersubjective sign systems. Whereas cognitivists adopt the first person perspective of epistemology (philosophy of the subject), semioticians adopt the third person perspective of the Language Analysis tradition.

Noam Chomsky and the Study of Competence

In the late fifties, the mind and cognition made a decisive return *within* the Language Analysis tradition, beginning with Noam Chomsky's transformational generative grammar (together with his decisive critique of B. F. Skinner's behaviorism).[38] In the form of Chomsky's linguistics, the Language Analysis tradition created a synthesis of both the mentalism of epistemology and the intersubjective nature of language, thus avoiding the idealism and first person perspective of epistemology and the (quasi) behaviorism of the Language Analysis tradition. In this respect, Chomsky's work represents the ideal paradigm for cognitive film semioticians.

David Bordwell has noted the absence of references to the work of Chomsky in film theory: "It is surprising that theorists who assign language a key role in determining subjectivity have almost completely ignored the two most important contemporary developments in linguistic theory: Chomsky's Transformational Generative Grammar and his Principles-and-Parameters theory."[39] He adds that "no film theorist has mounted an argument for *why* the comparatively informal theories of Saussure, Émile Benveniste, or Bakhtin are superior to the Chomskyan paradigm. For over two decades film theorists have made pronouncements about language without engaging with the major theoretical rival to their position."[40] The truth of the matter is that over the last two decades a number of film theorists have been engaging with Chomskyan linguistics and, furthermore, have deemed it to be superior to structural linguistics. Throughout this book I attempt to emphasize that Chomskyan linguistics, particularly in its study of competence, has defined the central doctrines of cognitive film semiotics. Here I shall briefly chart the relation between early film semiotics and cognitive film semiotics.

During the seventies, Metz's film semiotics was modified and transformed. Its fundamental problems, as we have already seen, lay in its total reliance upon structural linguistics. One major transformation came from post-structural film theory, which based itself primarily upon the Marxism of Louis Althusser and the psychoanalysis of Jacques Lacan. Post-structuralists criticize structuralism because they regard it to be the last vestige of Enlightenment reason and rationality. Christopher Norris clearly sums up this post-structural position:

Structuralism renounces the Kantian 'transcendental subject', only to re-place it with a kind of linguistic *a priori*, a regulative concept of 'structure' which seeks to place firm juridical limits on the play of signification. Such, at least, is the critique brought to bear upon structuralist thinking by those – like Lacan and Derrida – who read in it the last, lingering signs of a rationalist tradition forced up against its own (unconscious) limits.[41]

Ultimately, structuralism replaces the transcendental Kantian sub-ject with a transcendental signified.

For most Anglo-American film scholars, film semiotics takes only one form – namely, Metz's early film semiotics, ranging from his 1964 paper "Le cinéma: langue ou langage?" leading to his remarkable paper on the *grande syntagmatique* of the image track, and finally to his monumental book *Langage et cinéma*, published in 1971 and translated into English in 1974. But as Metz himself ac-knowledged in the opening chapter of this book, "By its very na-ture, the semiotic enterprise must expand or disappear."[42] Al-though *Langage et cinéma* marks the logical conclusion to Metz's structural linguistic–based film semiotics, it does not mark the end of film semiotics per se. In his subsequent work (particularly his essay "The Imaginary Signifier"),[43] Metz adopted a psychoanalyti-cal framework, which aided the formation of post-structural film theory. However, many of his students and colleagues continued to work within a semiotic framework, which they combined with cog-nitive science. Research in film semiotics continued unabated in the seventies, eighties, and nineties, especially in France, Italy, and the Netherlands. Far from disappearing, film semiotics has expanded into a new framework, one that overcomes the problems of struc-tural linguistic–based film semiotics by embracing three new theo-ries: (1) a renewed interest in enunciation theory in both film and television (particularly in the work of Francesco Casetti and Metz of *L'Énonciation impersonnelle ou le site du film*),[44] (2) pragmatics (in the work of Roger Odin), and (3) transformational generative gram-mar and cognitive science generally (in the work of Michel Colin and Dominique Chateau).

One defining characteristic of cognitive film semiotics is that it aims to model the actual mental activities (intuitive knowledge) involved in the making and understanding of filmic texts, rather than study filmic texts themselves. Ultimately, the theories of Fran-cesco Casetti, Roger Odin, Michel Colin, and Dominique Chateau are models of filmic competence. Each theorist models this competence from a slightly different perspective: Casetti employs the deictic theory of enunciation, Odin employs pragmatics, and Colin and Chateau employ generative grammar and cognitive science.

Chomsky's study of linguistic competence in his generative grammar (where 'grammar' is defined as a theory of language) is one of the main research programs that led to the development of cognitive science in the fifties. Generative grammar shifted linguistic inquiry away from epiphenomena (actual language behavior) and toward competence – the intuitive knowledge that underlies natural language behavior, together with the innate, biologically determined language faculty that constitutes this knowledge as species-specific. Chomsky therefore follows the Enlightenment philosophers' study of what distinguishes humans from non-humans. Chomsky defines the specificity of human reasoning in terms of the possession of a language faculty, a faculty that enables each human to internalize a particular natural language.

Generative grammar is therefore a cognitive theory of natural language. Its cognitive dimension consists of two stages: the study of the language faculty in its initial state and the study of this faculty after it has been conditioned by experience (which leads to the internalization of a particular natural language). The study of the language faculty in its initial state is called 'universal grammar' (the interlocutor's initial competence), whereas the study of a particular natural language involves accounting for the structure of the language faculty after it has been determined by experience (which leads to the formation of the interlocutor's attained competence).

To study the grammar of a particular natural language is to attain descriptive adequacy, whereas to study universal grammar is to attain explanatory adequacy. The aim of a descriptively adequate generative grammar is to construct a formal model (consisting of generative and transformational rules) that generates all and only the grammatical sentences of a particular natural language. By contrast, explanatory adequacy attempts to model the initial state of the language faculty, which Chomsky conceived in terms of a series of innate principles and parameters. If one studies English or Japanese grammar, one is studying the same language faculty (the same series of principles and parameters), but under different empirical conditions, conditions that set these principles and parameters in alternative configurations.

However, structural linguistics attains only observational adequacy, because it merely segments and classifies linguistic behavior into paradigms and does not attribute any cognitive reality to those paradigms. By contrast, Chomsky defines the language faculty and natural languages as cognitive realities, as physical components of the mind: "A generative grammar is not a set of statements about externalized objects constructed in some manner. Rather, it purports to depict exactly what one knows when one hears a language: that is, what has been learned, as supplemented by innate principles. UG [universal grammar] is a characterization of these innate, biologically determined principles, which constitute one component of the human mind – the language faculty."[45]

In its initial formation in the fifties and sixties, generative grammar attempted to distinguish itself from structural linguistics by defining itself as descriptively adequate, with little concern for explanatory adequacy. Descriptive adequacy was set out in what is known as the Standard Theory of generative grammar, as outlined by Chomsky in *Aspects of the Theory of Syntax*, published in 1965.[46] It is this early theory of generative grammar that the cognitive film semiotician Michel Colin used in his generative rereading of Metz's *grande syntagmatique*. In Chapter 5, I will outline both Chomsky's Standard Theory and Colin's re-reading of Metz.

I have noted that natural language is species-specific. But what exactly makes it species-specific? We have already seen that for Habermas it is through language that humans establish mutual understanding and coordinate social action. Chomsky refers to the property of discrete infinity (or the creativity principle); the structural linguist André Martinet refers to natural language's principle of economy, its doubly articulated system of organization.[47] For Chomsky and Martinet, natural language is distinctive because it generates infinite phenomena by finite means. Double articulation posits a first (the higher) level of language, analyzable into a large but finite number of meaningful units (morphemes, or monemes), and a second, lower level, consisting of a smaller number of non-meaningful units (phonemes), which have no semantic content in themselves but combine with one another on the higher level to form morphemes.[48] The morphemes in turn are combined in finite ways to produce an infinite number of sentences. Chomsky's Standard Theory comprises – much as semiotic models do – an underlying level of reality and a surface level. The underlying level consists of a finite number of base rules that generate a finite number of deep structures. These are then transformed into a potentially infinite number of surface structure sentences by the recursive application of a finite number of transformational rules. Chomsky's model of this underlying reality balances out language's limiting and enabling capacities.

Double articulation and discrete infinity can be made clearer by drawing an analogy with chess, which consists of a finite number of squares and a finite a number of chess pieces, each of which can be moved in a finite number of ways. But when we add up all these 'finites', we end up with a potentially infinite number of chess games.

A first justification for studying film in the context of generative linguistics is to discover whether it is also structured according to the property of discrete infinity. Initial signs are promising, since discrete infinity is premised on the ability to segment and classify the discrete units of a language, as Metz did successfully in constructing the *grande syntagmatique*. Discrete infinity is implicit in the *grande syntagmatique* to the extent that it formalizes the finite determined ordering (the eight images sequences) of an infinite number of undetermined units (shots).

Chapter Contents

Chapter 2 reviews the cognitive theories of George Lakoff and Mark Johnson, which are based on the premise that thought and language are represented in the mind in the form of schemata (cognitive structures that organize perceptual input into experiences) – more specifically, image schemata, which are directly motivated by bodily experience. The chapter outlines the notion of image schemata, and discusses the limitations of David Bordwell's non–image schemata theory of the film spectator, before moving on to consider the potential for developing a cognitive semantics of film from Michel Colin's essay "Film Semiology as a Cognitive Science," in which Colin perceives a close affinity between semiotics and cognitive science, since both paradigms address similar issues – language, vision, and problem solving. The chapter ends with my attempt to develop a cognitive semantics of film based on Lakoff's 'container' image schema.

Chapter 3 returns to the issue of filmic enunciation. Enunciation designates the activity that results in speech, in the production of utterances (*énoncés*). Émile Benveniste identified two forms of utterance: discourse (*discours*) and story (*histoire*). *Discours* employs words such as personal, possessive, and demonstrative pronouns that grammaticalize within the utterance particular aspects of its spatio-temporal context (e.g., the speaker and hearer), whereas *histoire* is a form of utterance that excludes pronouns. The cognitive film semiotician Francesco Casetti takes to its logical conclusions the analysis of film in terms of personal pronouns. Using the categories *I*, *you*, and *he*, he develops a typology of four shot types, which aims to describe the way film orients itself in relation to the spectator. However, Casetti also took the translinguistic framework to its logical conclusion and was rightly criticized by Metz for doing so. In his final published work (*L'Énonciation impersonnelle ou le site du film*), Metz disputes Casetti's pronoun theory of film arguing that film can only be studied as *histoire*. After criticizing Casetti's translinguistics, Metz did not expand the enunciative theory of film to incorporate general cognitive and ecological principles; instead, he simply replaced personal pronouns with anaphora – a narrow system of orientation in which one textual element points to another. Moreover, Metz identifies anaphora as a reflexive moment in a film, an identification that results in his identifying filmic enunciation with reflexivity. The terms of the debate between Casetti and Metz take up most of Chapter 3, although toward the end I attempt to argue that, in rejecting a translinguistic theory of filmic enunciation (one based exclusively on personal pronouns), we do not need to reject the indispensable concept of 'deixis', which designates a mechanism that orients individuals in relation to their environment. The personal pronouns of natural language constitute the privileged category of orientation, which has led many film theorists erroneously to equate deixis with pronouns. At the end of Chapter 3, I briefly develop a non-linguistic theory of deixis in film and television, by considering the issue of colorization of black and white films, as well as television viewers' comprehension of news programs.

In linguistics, cognitive pragmatics designates a discipline that describes a type of linguistic competence that governs the relation between utterances and the appropriate contexts in which they are uttered. Cognitive pragmatics is therefore a study of the immediate discursive nature of language. In Chapter 4 we see that, for the cognitive film semiotician Roger Odin, film semiotics is primarily pragmatic, because of the immediate discursive nature of film. According to Metz, film is a *"langage sans langue,"* that is, belongs to the dimension of *la parole*. Unlike for Saussure, for Odin *la parole* is not an heterogeneous domain of unconstrained language use, but is determined by a pragmatic competence. Odin develops a threefold distinction between institutions, modes, and operations in order to characterize the film spectator's pragmatic competence in comprehending films. This chapter charts the different institutions, modes, and operations specified in Odin's work and discusses in detail fiction films, documentaries, home movies, and what Odin calls the 'dynamic' mode of filmmaking.

Michel Colin made explicit the connection between film and generative grammar's concept of discrete infinity (as well as other concepts). In his essay "The Grande Syntagmatique Revisited," discussed in Chapter 5, Colin redefined the observationally adequate *grande syntagmatique* as descriptively adequate. This involved redefining the eight syntagmatic types in terms of selectional (or semantic) features. Selectional features represent the inherent grammatical and semantic components of lexical items (what the rest of humanity calls 'words'). For example, the lexical item 'cat' can be represented in terms of the following selectional features: +Common, +Count, +Animate, −Human. Every lexical item can be characterized in terms of these and other selectional features. If we return to the chess analogy, we can also analyze each chess piece into selectional features. This would simply involve encoding the 'grammatical' and 'semantic' components of each chess piece – the moves it can perform – in terms of a finite series of components. The most remarkable result of Colin's re-reading of Metz's work is that, as with all generative models, the actual, manifest syntagmatic types are posited as merely the result (the epiphenomenon) of the generative process. Within the generative framework, we can identify and analyze, not only actual syntagmas, but also possible (i.e., potential) syntagmas and impossible syntagmas. Once all the finite selectional features have been identified, the potentially infinite number of syntagmatic types can be conceived and generated. These selectional features constitute the finite underlying level of filmic discourse (or its system of codes) from which a potentially infinite number of film sequences can be generated. For Colin, then, the primary aim of the *grande syntagmatique* is not to identify actual syntagmatic types, but to identify the more fundamental selectional features that combine to form these syntagmatic types. Chapter 5 ends by using Colin's work as a starting point for thinking through and redefining the problem of the grammar of film in cognitive terms. Reference is also made to the work of Dominique Chateau and the American John M. Carroll.

All the cognitive film semioticians studied in this book are united by the same project – to combine film semiotics and cognitive science with the aim of modelling filmic competence. The following chapters offer my own sympathetic, but not entirely uncritical, working through of this project. Throughout, the reader may detect a tension between the need simply to present a project almost unknown to Anglo-American film scholars (in the interests of being informative, to make known what has been marginalized in Anglo-American film studies) and the need to develop my own elaboration of a (necessarily) fragmentary and incomplete project. As film semiotics has been marginalized and repressed in film studies, perhaps we could for a moment take the notion of working through in its Freudian sense (*Durcharbeitung*) and suggest that this book aims to overcome the resistance to film semiotics by returning it from the repressed. Once it is returned to consciousness, the reader may be surprised to find that what was repressed has, during its latency period, matured and been transformed into a new object.

CHAPTER TWO

The Body on Screen and in Frame

Film and Cognitive Semantics

> Reason is embodied in the sense that the very structures on which
> reason is based emerge from our bodily experiences. Reason is
> imaginative in the sense that it makes use of metonymies, meta-
> phors, and a wide variety of image schemas. (George Lakoff).[1]

Modern (or 'contemporary') film theory marks a decisive break with the classical film theory of Rudolf Arnheim, André Bazin, Bela Balàsz, Siegfried Kracauer, and Victor
Perkins. We can characterize this break as a transition from an
extensional semantic to an intensional (or immanent) semantic theory of meaning. Classical film theory is a theory of cinematic representation premised upon mechanical duplication (upon the existential relation between film and referent) and is therefore based
upon an extensional semantic theory of meaning. In contrast, modern film theory, beginning with the film semiotics of Christian
Metz, corresponds to an intensional semantic theory of meaning,
for it drove a wedge between mechanical duplication and cinematic
representation and then defined the latter, not externally – as the
effect of an existential link between film and referent – but internally – as an effect of codes.

Furthermore, the evolution of modern film theory can be characterized as progressing from an intensional semantic to a pragmatic theory of filmic meaning. Pragmatists study how successful
communication is achieved on the level of language use. This is
because, they argue, language's meaning is not determined in advance of its use. In the early days of pragmatic theory, deictic words
such as personal and demonstrative pronouns became the privileged example of how language only gains meaning when used.
For instance, the meaning of the personal pronoun 'I' is dependent
on the person uttering it at the time of speaking. For pragmatists,

language is structured around, and gains its meaning from, external absent causes (such as the speaker), and the purpose of early theories of pragmatics was to study how these external absent causes are formally represented in linguistic structure. In the seventies this early theory entered modern film theory through Emile Benveniste's theory of enunciation. In particular, the modern film theorists used Benveniste's theory of enunciation to argue that narrative film is structured around, and gains its meaning from, the external absent centre that spectators come to occupy. Within this theory the spectator is regarded as being formally represented in the film by the 'subject position' (traced onto the filmic image by means of the perspectival-optical system of the camera and reproduced across potentially disruptive cuts by means of conventions of spatial construction, such as the 180 degree rule, eyeline matches, and so on). The modern film theorists went beyond Benveniste's purely linguistic theory by conceiving the subject position in terms of Louis Althusser's theory of interpellation and Jacques Lacan's theory of the mirror phase.

In the previous chapter I pointed out the main problem with these theories – their implicit behaviorism, in which the spectator is theorized as passive, with no cognitive capacity to process information. Furthermore, it is a common assumption of psychoanalytic film theory that the cinema projects the spectator into a spatio-temporal elsewhere. That is, cinema releases the spectator from her immediate spatio-temporal limits by transporting her vision through space and time (while keeping the body motionless). Psychoanalytic film theory in effect dematerializes the spectator's body while privileging the unconscious mind and vision. This follows Descartes, who also disembodied vision by making it a property of the (conscious) mind. My aim in this chapter is to develop my own theory of cinematic perception, one that grounds perception in the physicality of the body. To achieve this I summarize the film theories of Metz, David Bordwell, and especially Michel Colin; identify their limitations (specifically relating to the disembodiment of perception); and attempt to overcome these limitations by reviewing and deploying George Lakoff's and Mark Johnson's cognitive semantic theory of meaning, a theory that extends and reformulates some of the basic assumptions of the Language Analysis tradition.

Disembodied Structures and Schemata in Film Theory: Metz, Bordwell, Colin

Saussure's principle of the arbitrary and conventional relation between signifier and signified implies a disembodied realm of conceptual structure (the signified), since the body is not seen to motivate the meaning of signifiers. To sustain the theory of the arbitrary sign, Saussure developed the concept of a language as an underlying system, because the sign consists of the combination of two entities without connection, and only a system, consisting of necessary conventions, can explain how the signifier and signified are combined.

In "Cinema: Language or Language System?"[2] Metz failed to establish a film semiotics on the level of the image because of his inability to articulate a new epistemological position on film by means of the notion of the arbitrary relation between signifier and signified, for he believed the filmic image to be motivated. In order to achieve his primary aim – to define filmic specificity in semiotic terms – Metz sought, in "Problems of Denotation in the Fiction Film,"[3] arbitrariness on the level of image sequences, which confer upon the profilmic events a meaning that *goes beyond* their analogical relation to the image. These image sequences conform to the principle of arbitrariness because there is no strict motivation governing the choice of one image sequence over another in representing a particular profilmic event.

In "Cinema: Language or Language System?" and "Problems of Denotation in the Fiction Film," Metz worked with the conception of the image-as-analogue (as a mechanical duplication of reality). Stephen Heath called this "the blind spot of Metz's formulations," for it is "the point at which the articulation of significance collapses in the face of analogy."[4] But in *Language and Cinema*, Metz overcame this blind spot under the influence of Umberto Eco. Eco was one of the first semioticians to study the image successfully in terms of codes; that enabled him to define its apparent analogical (non-semiotic) nature as a system of iconic codes organized into a triple hierarchy.[5]

The basic terms that Metz worked with were therefore arbitrariness, motivation, code, and iconicity. Arbitrariness is opposed to motivation and is correlated with code, whereas code is opposed to iconicity and is correlated with arbitrariness (although in *Language and Cinema* Metz defined iconicity in terms of codes).[6] Metz began from the folk psychological premise that film is motivated and iconic, then proceeded to demonstrate that it is in fact coded and conforms to the principle of arbitrariness. Furthermore, structural linguistics begins from the premise that language is a system of uninterpreted (meaningless) symbols. For structural linguistics, meaning arises out of non-meaning, from the combination of phonemes (which have no semantic content, but only signify difference) into morphemes (which do have semantic content).

In *Narration in the Fiction Film* David Bordwell rejected a theory of film based on structural linguistics and instead developed a schema-based theory of filmic comprehension. Cognitive psychologists define schemata as abstract, transcendental, static, top-down (rather than bottom-up) structures of the mind that organize perceptual input into coherent mental representations.[7] Schemata are therefore finite abstract structures that interact with an infinite amount of perceptual data to form experiences. In this sense, schemata constitute the generative capacity of the mind to comprehend perceptions recurrently. Bordwell develops his theory within the Constructivist school of cognitive psychology, which studies the activity of the perceiver in generating hypotheses and inferences in order to make sense of inherently fragmentary and incomplete perceptual input. From this perspective, Bordwell conceptualizes the narrative film as an inherently incomplete form of discourse (as with all other forms of discourse). More specifically, he argued that the narrative film's logical form is incomplete, but is enriched, or completed, by the spectator's activity of inference generation.

Narrative film conforms to a psychologically motivated cause-effect logic. Bordwell describes this logic in terms of the two tier *fabula-syuzhet* opposition as formulated by the Russian Formalists:

Presented with two narrative events, we look for causal or spatial or temporal links. The imaginary construct we create, progressively and retrospectively, was termed by Formalists the *fabula* (sometimes translated as "story"). More specifically, the fabula embodies the action as a chronological, cause-and-effect chain of events occuring within a given duration and spatial field. . . . The *syuzhet* (usually translated as "plot") is the actual arrangement and presentation of the fabula in the film. It is not the text in toto. It is a more abstract construct, the patterning of a story as a blow-by-blow recounting of the film could render it.[8]

In constructing a fabula, the perceiver defines some phenomena as events while constructing relations among them. These relations are primarily causal ones. An event will be assumed to be a consequence of another event, of a character trait, or of some general law. The syuzhet can facilitate this process by systematically encouraging us to make linear casual inferences. But the syuzhet can also arrange events so as to block or complicate the construction of casual relations.[9]

To complete the film's narrative logic, the film spectator must possess a cause-effect schema that will serve as the context in which the narrative film is processed. The cause-effect schema is the context most accessible during the spectator's processing of a narrative film, for (in the terms of Sperber and Wilson's principle of relevance, discussed in Chapter 4) it enables the spectator to process the inherently incomplete logical form of the narrative film with the least amount of processing effort yielding an optimal contextual effect.

Bordwell's theory is primarily a top-down account of information processing; from this perspective, perceptual data (in this instance, narrative films) are conceived merely as a set of cues interacting with the spectator's cognitive capacity (in this instance, the cause-effect schema), triggering and constraining her activity of inference generation. In Bordwell's terms, the cues in the narrative film are organized in such a way as "to encourage the spectator to execute story construction activities. The film presents cues, patterns and gaps that shape the viewer's application of schemata and the testing of hypotheses."[10] The narrative film cues and constrains the story construction activities of the spectator in such a way as to enable her to form the space, time, and cause-effect dimensions of the film into a single, coherent mental representation.

The cause-effect schema constrains the film spectator to interpret the narrative film's set of cues in a particular way – in terms of a character-centred causality, based on the psychological motivations and rational actions of characters. The schema is, in effect, an interpretive strategy for the spectator, enabling her to recognize certain perceptual data as relevant cues, to generate the necessary inferences, and to combine cues and inferences into a coherent mental representation.

The result of the interface between narrative film and cause-effect schema – the film's fabula – is not a pre-existing entity, but a mental representation constructed by the spectator during her on-going experience of the film's syuzhet.[11] The spectator's construction of the fabula is therefore a procedural (rather than a static) process. The fabula is in a constant state of change, due to the spectator's ongoing generation of new inferences, strengthening of existing inferences, and abandonment of existing inferences.

The combined schemata plus procedural account of information processing accurately describe the Constructivist theory of perception, a theory Bordwell explicitly adopts. The strength of Constructivism for film studies lies precisely in its emphasis on the procedural, top-down, defeasible nature of the perceiver's activity in information processing.

I have discussed Bordwell at length here because he can be credited with pioneering a cognitive theory of filmic meaning. Yet recent advancements in cognitive theory inevitably reveal the limitations of Bordwell's theory: He conceives schemata as transcendental, functioning to construct literal meaning only, and isolates them from both language and the body. George Lakoff and Mark Johnson argue that schemata conceived in this way are static structures simply imposed upon perceptual input to give it meaning. Lakoff insists that such traditional theories of schemata attempt "to provide a format for representing human knowledge in computational models of the mind. They attempt to do so by providing conventional propositional structures in terms of which situations can be understood."[12] Because they only account for literal meaning, such theories exclude the imaginative projective devices that both Lakoff and Johnson posit as being fundamental to cognitive reasoning, devices such as metaphor and metonymy. As we shall see, both authors call for an enrichment of the theory of schemata, to move them away from a transcendental conception by taking into account imaginative projective devices, and also by conceiving them as dynamic, not static.

In contrast to Bordwell's, Lakoff's and Johnson's schemata are image-based, are embodied and inherently meaningful (are constituted by the structure of the body) rather than being transcendental, are based on metaphor and metonymy, and are dynamic rather than static. But such schemata are not made up of what we generally think of as mental images, since an image in this traditional sense always refers to particular objects and events. Instead, the emphasis remains with the term 'schema': Image schemata are non-representational spatial structures; they delineate the abstract structure of images.

Bordwell's cognitivism follows the philosophy of the subject in that both involve disembodiment and the subject's isolation from language. Firstly, in terms of disembodiment, Bordwell only considers the physiological characteristics of the eye when outlining his schema theory. Like Descartes, Bordwell connects the eye only to the mind, thereby separating both from the body. Secondly, Bordwell's isolation of language is evident in his rejection of a communication model of narration. He asks, "Must we go beyond the process of narration to locate an entity which is its source?"[13] and answers, "To give every film a narrator or implied author is to indulge in an anthropomorphic fiction. . . . [This strategy takes] the process of narration to be grounded in the classic communication diagram: a message is passed from sender to receiver."[14] As opposed to this communication model, Bordwell argues that narration "presupposes a perciever, but not any sender, of a message."[15]

By rejecting the narrator and the communication model of narration, Bordwell confers too much autonomy upon the spectator in constructing filmic meaning. More generally – and to express it in Habermas's terms – cognitivism assigns to the spectator a "narcissistically overinflated autonomy" and "purposively rational self-assertion." What this means is that cognitivism focuses on isolated, purposively acting subjects at the expense of intersubjective communicative practices. By contrast, Habermas (and the Language Analysis tradition generally) rightly stresses the need to conceive of subjects as necessarily bound up in intersubjective, communicative relationships, which involve reciprocal recognition and social interaction, made possible by language. In rejecting the narrator, Bordwell adheres to the 'first person perspective' of the philosophy of the subject, isolating the spectator from intersubjective, communicative relationships (the 'third person perspective' advanced by the Language Analysis tradition), which is fundamental to the coordination of social action in human society.

In "Film Semiology as a Cognitive Science"[16] the cognitive film semiotician Michel Colin begins by taking Metz's statement "to understand how film is understood"[17] as the central aim of film semiotics. This involves investigating the correspondence between semantics and visual representation, without falling into the trap of identifying semantics as specifically linguistic (the trap, Katz and Fodor argue, that Chomsky falls into). The alternative is to align semantics with conceptual structure (as do Katz and Fodor). For Colin, to approach the issue of how film is understood, cognitive film semiotics "must describe the rules governing the links between the visual representations of 3-D scenes and conceptual structures," a description that "largely implies the analysis of the links between shots."[18] This explains why Colin reread in great detail Metz's *grande syntagmatique*, primarily within Chomsky's Standard Theory of transformational generative grammar (see Chapter 5).

But in "Film Semiology as a Cognitive Science," Colin moves closer to the position of Katz and Fodor by employing the framework of non-linguistic domains of cognitive science (but without rejecting linguistics altogether, as we shall see). For Colin, Metz's view that the aim of film semiotics is to understand how film is understood presents film semiotics as being closely related to cognitive science, since (in Terry Winograd's definition) cognitive science specializes in research on language, vision, and problem solving. From this premise, Colin maintains that

there is no need to insist on the fact that film semiology is concerned with problems of vision and language; only the third field can seem unrelated to the semiological approach. It is, however, reasonable to consider that the interpretation of semantic phenomena, such a spatial-temporal relationships or co-reference, imply the solving of problems. Thus, it can be argued that the understanding of the shot-reverse shot implies a solution to the problem of determining the position of the characters within the diegetic space on the basis of the filmic configuration (alternation between two shots). More generally, it could be said that the codes postulated by the semiological approach are an explanation of the knowledge necessary to the solving of the problems raised by the interpretation of filmic configurations. For instance, a code such as the grande syntagmatique of narrative film can be considered to represent the knowledge that the spectator needs in order to solve the problems of spatio-temporal relationships within the image track.[19]

Colin's identification of filmic comprehension as a problem-solving activity enables him to posit his object of study as the spectator's active, cognitive processes that constitute filmic meaning. This cognitive conception of the film-spectator interface posits that the filmic text does not signify its own meaning, but is constituted by those spectators who possess the necessary knowledge.

Following Gilbert Ryle, cognitive scientists argue that comprehension involves two fundamental types of knowledge: declarative and procedural knowledge (i.e., 'knowing that' and 'knowing how', respectively).[20] One of the tasks of cognitive film semiotics is to identify the specific knowledge needed to understand cinematic language, and how spectators use that knowledge in the process of comprehension. Cognitive film semiotics therefore strives to describe the filmic intuitions of the ideal film spectator, to characterize what a film spectator knows when she is able to understand a film. Colin approaches this task by considering how artificial intelligence (AI) conceptualizes the representation of knowledge, which he considers under three headings:[21]

(a) Acquiring more knowledge
(b) Retrieving relevant facts from knowledge
(c) Reasoning about the facts in search of a solution

I shall outline and extend Colin's discussion of these categories.

Acquiring More Knowledge. Category (a) involves the relation between knowledge that is given and that which is new. Colin argues that film semiotics has previously concentrated only on given knowledge – that is, has never considered how knowledge (both given and new) is acquired. Colin refers to the notion of encyclopedic competence, a term deriving from the distinction between the encyclopedia and the dictionary.[22] But such a conception is based almost entirely on declarative knowledge. That is, encyclopedic knowledge, consisting of a series of interconnections between manifest chunks of information, does not take into account the active, generative capacity of the mind. But recent research into knowledge and cognition has shifted emphasis toward the dynamic, generative workings of the mind. For example, in a discussion of their principle of relevance, Dan Sperber and Deirdre Wilson argue that "people have not only the knowledge that they actually entertain, but also the knowledge that they are capable of deducing from the knowledge that they entertain."[23] For Sperber and Wilson, an individual does not have to be aware of all her knowledge (an assumption implicit in the encyclopedia model of knowledge), since an individual's knowledge consists of what she knows together with the generative capacities that allows her to generate additional knowledge from what she knows. And the individual is not aware of this additional knowledge until it is generated.

In order to advance on the question of given/new knowledge, film semiotics needs to shift its emphasis to procedural aspects of knowledge and must also identify mechanisms of knowledge generation and acquisition.

Retrieving Relevant Facts from Knowledge. Category (b) is dependent on how knowledge is organized. Colin refers to semantic networks (a hierarchy of levels of knowledge, from general to specific) and to frames and scripts (both of which are types of schemata). But again, these are static, declarative models of knowledge. In Sperber and Wilson's dynamic model, the retrieval of knowledge also involves the generation of knowledge, as the following example shows:

> Suppose Mary and Peter are looking at a landscape where she has noticed a distant church. She says to him,
> (49) I've been inside that church
> She does not stop to ask herself whether he has noticed the building, and whether he assumes she has noticed, and assumes she has noticed he has noticed, and so on, or whether he has assumed it is a church, and assumes she assumes it is, and so on. All she needs is reasonable confidence that he will be able to identify the building as a church when required to: in other words, that a certain assumption will be manifest in his cognitive environment at the right time.[24]

Sperber and Wilson are arguing against the mutual knowledge hypothesis, which states that, in order for the receiver to retrieve the same meaning from the message as that encoded by the sender, the sender and receiver must not only share the same system of codes, but know that they share this system. Mutual knowledge is therefore knowledge that is shared and known to be shared. But knowing that the knowledge is shared leads to an infinite regress, or an infinite process of checking. In the preceding example, for the knowledge that the building is a church to be mutually known, Mary must know that Peter knows that the building is a church, and Peter must know that Mary knows that the building is a church. But then, Mary must know that Peter knows that she (Mary) knows that the building is a church, and Peter must know that Mary knows that he (Peter) knows that the building is a church, and so on. For mutual knowledge to be established, Mary and Peter must not only know the same knowledge, but must know that they share this knowledge, and know that they know that they share this knowledge, and so on ad infinitum.[25] It is the psychological unreality of the mutual knowledge hypothesis that makes it implausible, and it seems that the static, encyclopedic model of knowledge is also based upon the mutual knowledge hypothesis.

Reasoning about the Facts in Search of a Solution. In category (c), Colin refers to procedural knowledge – to ways in which facts are processed by individuals. As well as procedures, Colin also mentions the following strategies: analogy, formalization, generalization, and abstraction. Lakoff and Johnson have reduced these processes down to two – metaphor and metonymy – whereas Sperber and Wilson have identified one process – the principle of relevance. Colin attempts to overcome the lack of procedural knowledge processes in film semiotics in an analysis of an ideal spectator's comprehension of spatial relations in a scene from *The Barefoot Contessa* (Joseph Mankiewicz). To do this he employs (without introducing) the 'general space planner' (GSP) of Charles M. Eastman,[26] an early attempt at computer aided design. It is a computer program designed to overcome space planning problems – the organization and arrangement of objects (furniture, wall partitions, etc.) within a bounded space. The program contains the necessary number of constraints (the distance needed between furniture, locations where furniture cannot be placed, and so on), and is asked to compute the optimal solution.

The appeal of the GSP in explaining how spectators mentally construct filmic space should be obvious. The GSP is a procedural process explicitly constructed as a problem-solving activity. By using the GSP, Colin imputes that each spectator's construction of filmic space is a problem-solving activity, in which filmic space is gradually pieced together by the spectator, who is following a series of constraints. Such constraints correspond to the rules of continuity editing. Failure to construct a coherent space will be due to ill-defined constraints (either an insufficient number or contradictory constraints), or by the spectator's improperly locating a shot within the bounded space (the film scene). But the more the constraints are well defined, the more efficient the construction of the bounded space will be.

The scene Colin analyzes occurs near the beginning of the film, as four characters enter a cabaret (the bounded space) and sit around a table. Much of the scene consists of shots depicting one character only, so the spatial position of each character in relation to the others needs to be worked out (and reinforced) by each spectator in a procedural manner. Colin notes: "It can then be assumed that the spectator goes through the mental process of reconstructing the spatial relationships between the characters on the basis of successive shots of each one."[27] Colin also mentions that the entrance and the table serve as stable anchoring points of the scene, even though they are not shown at the same time.

The general process Colin is examining is that of constructing a coherent mental representation of what is not actually experienced in toto – the spatial layout of the cabaret, together with the four characters sitting around a table. Colin argues that, once a spectator has mentally constructed this space, a few contradictory cues (such as the breaking of the 180 degree rule) can be rectified, since it stands out as an anomaly (or the contradictory cues can be said to be displaced codes that leave traces of their original position). However, it is possible that a series of contradictory cues will force the spectator to revise her mental representation of the scene.

As does Bordwell, therefore, Colin acknowledges that comprehension is a procedural, top-down, defeasible process continually under review. The spectator is ceaselessly attempting to solve problems when watching a film – constructing the optimal filmic space (and, of course, time and narrative) from the cues offered by the text. Colin and Bordwell differ only in the way this process is theorized. Although Colin moves into non-linguistic areas of cognitive science, he does not reject linguistics as a paradigm for film studies. At the end of "Film Semiology as a Cognitive Science," he addresses the issue of the relation between cognitive and linguistic faculties. In effect, the debate is between modular and non-modular theories of the mind. The modular view is advocated most strongly by Jerry Fodor,[28] who posits a theory of the mind consisting of separate cognitive domains (or input systems) with the following properties: Each system is 'domain-specific' (it specializes in processing a particular type of stimulus only), 'innately specified' (i.e., it is not learnt, but already known); 'hardwired' (it can be associated with neural systems), and 'autonomous' (it does not share memory, attention, and so on, with other cognitive systems).[29] No module has access to information in other parts of the mind, including those containing general cognitive abilities. For Fodor, grammar is a module whose sole domain is the processing of linguistic input; as such, it is insensitive to all other cognitive capacities.

Bordwell implicitly adopts at least a number of the tenets of the modular theory of the mind – especially the domain-specific and autonomous nature of information processing. In *Narration in the Fiction Film* he states: "It will come as no surprise that I do not treat the spectator's operations as necessarily modeled upon linguistic activities."[30] Furthermore, he does not consider the rhetorical tropes of metaphor and metonymy to be relevant to the construction and comprehension of the film's fabula, since he considers metaphor and metonymy to be linguistic tropes.[31]

But for Colin: "As far as film semiology is concerned, the problem is then knowing whether the homologies between linguistic and filmic structures depend on linguistic faculties, or derive from the fact that language and film call for the same mental faculties."[32] Colin confronts this issue by quoting Ray Jackendoff's claim "There is a *single* level of mental representation, *conceptual structure*, at which linguistic, sensory, and motor information are compatible."[33] This view of the mind then allows for the possibility that linguistic structure interacts (i.e., is compatible) with visual data, that language does have a role to play in the mental processing of nonlinguistic information. Jackendoff calls this the 'cognitive constraint': "There must be levels of mental representation at which information conveyed by language is compatible with information from peripheral systems such as vision, nonverbal audition, smell, kinesthesia, and so forth. If there were no such levels, it would be impossible to use language to report sensory input. We couldn't talk about what we see and hear."[34] But this is not to advocate a return to the translinguistics of the sixties, of reducing all semiotics to linguistic meaning, far less advocating substantive parallels between film and language.

Bordwell's (untheorized) modular view of the mind forecloses on questions of the role of language in the processing of filmic texts. It seems that he has adopted this position on the basis of his criticism of past results on the application of linguistic concepts to film.[35] But even if all of Bordwell's criticisms were justified, this does not, a priori, rule out the applicability of other linguistic concepts to film. The problem with Bordwell's cognitivism is that he has rejected the communication model of narration, the role of the narrator, and has developed a disembodied theory of schemata. Colin's cognitive film semiotics avoids the first two problems by remaining within a communicative framework, although he does not take into consideration the role of the body in filmic comprehension.

Cognitive Semantics

In his essay "Semiotic Foundations of the Cognitive Paradigm,"[36] Winfried Nöth considers the affinities between semiotics and cognitive science. Nöth asks, "Is semiotics one of the paradigms that have been replaced by cognitive science, has the cognitive turn in the humanities resulted in a paradigm shift within semiotics, or has semiotics remained unaffected by the cognitive turn?"[37] Nöth goes on to argue that the paradigms cannot simply be compared and contrasted since there are many forms of cognitivism just as there are many schools of semiotics. Nonetheless, Nöth does argue that, although cognitive science has many affinities with Peircean semiotics, it has very little in common with Saussurean semiotics. This is particularly evident when he compares Saussurean semiotics to George Lakoff's experientialist view of cognition, which is based on the premise that thought and language are fundamentally motivated by bodily experience.

Lakoff's view is shared by a growing number of researchers who study the interface between cognitive science and linguistics – including Mark Johnson, Mark Turner, Ronald Langacker, Gilles Fauconnier, and Eve Sweester.[38] (It is generally regarded that George Lakoff and Mark Johnson are the dominant representatives of cognitive semantics, so I shall focus on them.) Lakoff and Johnson trace the origins of intangible abstract thought back to the body, rather than consider thought to exist in an autonomous realm. They therefore challenge what is known within Western philosophy as 'objectivism'.

One dominant issue that marks the difference between objectivism and cognitive semantics is that of 'mental representation'. Whereas objectivists believe that knowledge is represented in the mind by propositions consisting of meaningless symbols (which gain their meaning via a direct correspondence to external reality), cognitive semantics posits that knowledge is represented in the mind in the form of schemata (cognitive structures that organize perceptual input into experiences). More specifically, cognitive semanticists such as Lakoff and Johnson have posited a series of *image* schemata that structure perceptual input into experiences. These schemata are inherently meaningful because they gain their meaning directly from the body's innate sensory-motor capacities. Image schemata therefore represent 'the body in the mind' (to use the title of Johnson's book) and are posited as being cognitively real because they are directly motivated (non-arbitrary) and inherently meaningful. Cognitive semantics therefore challenges the dualism (the mind-body problem) of Cartesian philosophy. Descartes defined the body as a machine determined by mechanical laws, which can be described by means of the principles of mechanics. But introspection reveals that the mind cannot be described in the same way. Descartes therefore posited the mind to be made up of a second material (*res cogitans*, or thinking substance), which is not reducible to the principles of mechanics. It is this second substance that distinguishes humans from non-humans, according to Descartes. But if the mind and body are two completely separate substances, how do they interact? This dualism, one of the dominant principles of objectivism, is overcome in cognitive semantics by establishing a determinate link between the body and cognition. In effect, cognitive semantics mediates between dualism and its polar opposite, eliminative behaviorism, which repudiates the existence of any mental events or states by reducing them to bodily behavior. In rejecting both dualism and eliminative behaviorism, cognitive semantics defines itself as a form of mental materialism, in which mental phenomena are dependent on (or are realized by) the material (the body), but are not mechanically reducible to the material.

The problem both Lakoff and Johnson have with objectivism is that it bypasses humans. Reasoning is believed to be based entirely on propositional structure and literal meaning operating autonomously from human experiences, with little or no room for image schemata that gain their meaning from (or are directly motivated by) the body, and imaginative processes of thinking, such as metaphor and metonymy. The objectivist approach conceives cognition to be transcendental and abstract – as disembodied, a premise that perpetuates the Cartesian mind-body problem, as we have already seen (a problem, incidentally, maintained by cognitivists who study the mind as a computer). Lakoff and Johnson instead emphasize the human nature of the mind and cognition – or, more specifically, argue that cognition is embodied. Lakoff writes that "where objectivism defines meaning independently of the nature and experience of thinking beings, experiential realism characterizes meaning in terms of *embodiment*, that is, in terms of our collective biological capacities and our physical and social experiences as beings functioning in our environment."[39] Lakoff is using a broad definition of the term 'experience', one that includes everything that plays a role in constructing human understanding, from the genetic makeup of our bodies to the way the body interacts with its social environment. Lakoff stresses that this is not simply a return to classical empiricism, in which experience is understood as passively received sense impressions, since "experience does not *determine* conceptual systems, but only *motivates* them."[40] Johnson similarly rejects the classical empiricist definition of experience, defining it instead in socio-historical terms.[41]

To specify what they mean by embodiment, Lakoff and Johnson make the distinction between conceptual structure and preconceptual bodily experiences and employ the notion of embodiment to argue that conceptual structure arises from (or is motivated by) preconceptual bodily experiences. The distinction is not therefore based on the opposition between structured concepts and unstructured experiences, for both authors argue that experience is itself structured and is already meaningful.

Lakoff and Johnson's cognitive semantics therefore challenges a number of the basic assumptions of the Language Analysis tradition. Firstly, cognitive semantics presents a striking alternative to the structural linguistic assumptions that the sign is arbitrary and that meaning arises out of non-meaning. Secondly, Lakoff developed cognitive grammar from generative semantics, which he helped to formulate in the sixties. Briefly, generative semantics was a response to Noam Chomsky's Standard Theory of Transformational Generative Grammar (outlined in Chapter 5). Generative semantics took many of its premises from the Standard Theory but refuted the claim that the deep structure is a formalized system of uninterpreted (meaningless) symbols that later receive a semantic interpretation. For the generative semanticists, the deep structure *is* the semantic interpretation (is already meaningful). Lakoff's cognitive semantics discards all traces of transformational grammar to develop the idea that language is already meaningful and is motivated by bodily experiences. This emphasis on bodily experiences is also adopted by Johnson, although he refers to his position as descriptive or empirical phenomenology.[42]

Lakoff characterizes experience in terms of kinesthetic image schemata, which are simple structures that arise from the body – up–down, back–front, centre–periphery, part–whole, inside–outside, paths, links, forces, and so on. These schemata are directly constrained by the dimensions of the human body. And because the dimensions of the fully grown body are shared (uniform and constant), any discussion of conceptual structure in terms of the body does not fall into radical relativism and subjectivism. Image schemata are not, therefore, arbitrary, but are directly motivated by a shared and constant bodily experience.

The structure of our shared bodily experience then becomes the basis for rational, abstract thought by means of image based schemata and creative strategies such as metaphor and metonymy, which project and extend this structure from the physical domain into the abstract domain of concepts. As Johnson observes: "Through metaphor, we can make use of patterns that obtain in our physical experience to organize our more abstract understanding"[43] (examples are provided later).

The basic premises of experientialism are represented schematically in Figure 3. This figure shows that what is taken to be an autonomous realm in objectivism (conceptual structure) is shown in experientialism to be the end result of a series of processes. We see that preconceptual experience is constituted by image schemata. Lakoff outlines several kinesthetic image schemata and shows how they determine the structure of abstract conceptual thought:[44]

1. The container schema, which structures our fundamental awareness of our bodies, is based on the elements 'interior', 'boundary', and 'exterior'. In terms of metaphorical extension, Lakoff notes that the visual field is commonly conceived as a container, since things 'come into' and 'go out of' sight. Also our understanding of our emergence out of various states of mind (drunkenness, dizziness, and so on) is also a metaphorical extension of the container schema. Theories are commonly understood as containers – for example, we say that a theory is watertight, or cannot

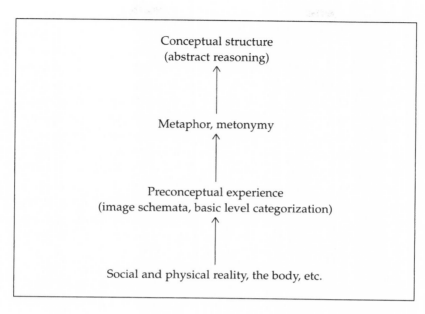

Conceptual structure
(abstract reasoning)

↑

Metaphor, metonymy

↑

Preconceptual experience
(image schemata, basic level categorization)

↑

Social and physical reality, the body, etc.

Fig. 3

hold water, or we refer to a theory's *frame*work (as we shall see, the frame as container is fundamental in the comprehension of films). Sometimes, theories are understood in terms of a particular type of container, a building: For example, we commonly say that a theory has no foundations, needs shoring up, has collapsed, and so on.

Johnson calls the container schema the in–out schema, structured on our physical experience of our bodies as both containers and as objects that can be contained.[45] However, these two schemata are not identical: The in–out schema has a broader scope, defining the boundary between what is contained (in) and what is excluded from the container (out).

2. The part–whole schema, also fundamental to our self-awareness, is based on our perception of our bodies as wholes made up of parts. It is extended in numerous ways, by metaphorical projection, into the realm of abstract thought. Lakoff mentions that families are understood in terms of the part–whole schema.

3. The link schema is based on our awareness of our position in relation to others, in which this sense of position enables us to establish a link between self and other. Social and interpersonal relations are metaphorically conceived in terms of 'making con-

nections' or 'breaking social ties', whereas freedom is understood as the absence of any links 'tying us down'.

4. The centre–periphery schema is similar to the part–whole schema in that it is based on our awareness of our bodies as having centres (the trunk and internal organs) and peripheries (limbs, hair, etc.). The centre gains its importance from the basic fact that the preservation of the body is more important to survival than the peripheries. Again, many abstract entities (such as theories) are metaphorically understood in terms of this schema.

5. The source-path-goal schema is based on our experience of bodily movement in a particular direction from one point to another along a path. Its many metaphorical extensions include its structuring of one's long-term aims and ambitions, which become 'sidetracked' or 'blocked' by obstacles.

In addition to covering some of these schemata, Johnson discusses the balance schema. As are other image schemata, it is based upon our bodily experience (a symmetry of forces relative to an axis) and can be metaphorically mapped onto other domains to give them structure. Johnson considers how balance operates in visual artworks and other phenomena (including theoretical arguments) that are understood in terms of balance. Whereas our bodily sense of balance is based upon gravitational and physical forces, in artworks this physical bodily experience is metaphorically mapped onto vision (and in theoretical arguments, balance is mapped onto concepts). From the balance schema, cognitive semantics is able to answer the question why symmetry and balance are pleasing in artworks – because they imitate the symmetry and balance of the perceiver's body. The process of reasoning and comprehension can be described using Lakoff's theory of experientialism in terms of the ability to form complex concepts by projecting several image schemata into the conceptual domain.

A Cognitive Semantics of Film

In this final section, I want to go beyond the work of Metz, Bordwell, and Colin by developing a cognitive semantic theory of film – one that takes into consideration the role of the body in filmic perception. In applying Lakoff and Johnson to film, I want to refer to Figure 3 and emphasize that the causality is not just one way.

That is, abstract reasoning is not merely an effect of bodily experience, since I shall argue that abstract reasoning (or, in this
instance, comprehension of a film) changes the way we experience
our bodies.

A general point that needs to be repeated about image schemata
is that they are "directly meaningful, since they put us in touch
with preconceptual structures in our bodily experience of functioning in the world."[46] Just as kinesthetic image schemata are not
arbitrary, but are directly motivated by (and directly obtain their
meaning from) bodily experience, so the metaphorical projection of
image schemata onto conceptual structure is also motivated by
bodily experience. Here we see Lakoff and Johnson eliminating the
semiotic principle of arbitrariness from the fundamental processes
of meaning and cognition.

How are the metaphorical projection processes of meaning employed in film viewing? I shall limit myself to discussing what I
consider to be the most fundamental kinesthetic image schemata
relevant to the comprehension of film – the container (and in-out)
schema.

Whereas in daylight we are able us to orient our bodies in
relation to the environment (since we can perceive distance, depth,
extension, surface, and so on), in the dark we become disoriented,
because we cannot perceive distance between us and the environment. This breaking down of the relation between self and other
affects ego boundaries, as Eugene Minkovski points out:

[Dark space] does not spread out before me but touches me directly, envel-
ops me, embraces me, even penetrates me, completely passes through me,
so that one can almost say that while the ego is permeable by darkness it
is not permeable by light. The ego does not affirm itself in relation to
darkness but becomes confused with it, becomes one with it. In this way
we become aware of a major difference between our manners of living
light space and dark space.[47]

This means that, in the dark, the individual's consciously experienced tactile body image can no longer function as the basis for
meaning, since it cannot establish a relation to its environment. In
the darkened auditorium, the bright, delimited screen serves to
'rescue' the spectator's tactile body image; it re-engages the spectator's body, offers it a stable reference point, and returns the body
to its role of generating meaning. As perceived in the auditorium,

a film works against the darkness that surrounds it. Correlatively, each spectator seeks out the bright image on screen in order to become oriented and to create a meaningful environment again. Unlike everyday life outside the cinema, the darkness of the auditorium works in a superlative manner to engage each spectator's body image, and thus her kinesthetic image schemata.

It is not, of course, only the darkness that primes the spectator – it is also the screen, frame, narrative structure, and the process of suture. These terms form the basis of the modern film theorists' concept of subject positioning. Crucial to this concept is the film's frame, which serves to fix the spectator's attention to the filmic image projected on screen. It achieves this by determining the boundary between what is included and what is excluded from the spectator's vision at any one moment. The function of the frame is therefore literally to position the spectator in a spatial relation to the image, fixing her visual and aural attention on screen.[48] Stephen Heath, one of the most prominent of the modern film theorists, then metaphorically mapped the function of the frame onto narrative. (Like Lakoff and Johnson, therefore, Heath begins with a literal, spatial experience, then metaphorically maps this onto the abstract domain of narrative.) Heath argues that narrative is "a decisive instance of framing in film," since it "*checks* the images, centring and containing, prescribing a reading as correlation of actions and inscribing a subject as, and for, the coherence of that operation, carried through against possible dispersion, the multiple intensities of the text of the film."[49] Heath's main model here is a tension between containment and dispersion – a containment of excess carried out by means of frame and narrative, which in their turn ensure a stable subject position (now understood in both literal and metaphorical terms).[50]

In cognitive semantic terms, basic filmic comprehension consists of the automatic projection onto film (filmic space and time, as well as narrative) of preconceptual kinesthetic image schemata, by means of metaphor and metonymy, forming the film's basic structure and level of meaning. This process primarily involves the projection of image schemata onto vision, which engages the image on screen. Some of the schemata are invariant (in-out, container schemata), whereas others are variant (such as source-path-goal). In the final pages of this chapter I shall begin applying the container schema to the cinema.

We have seen that Heath has already used the term 'containment' when theorizing subject positioning in terms of both frame and narrative. Using Lakoff's container schema, I shall explore both the frame and the diegesis. To say that the frame and diegesis are understood in terms of a kinesthetic image schema is to suggest that they are comprehended in terms of our experience of our bodies as containers. The frame in particular is analogous to (or is a reduplication of) sight itself, which, as Lakoff remarks, is also understood in terms of the container schema. But before discussing frame and diegesis, it is necessary to contextualize them. The term 'diegesis' was first introduced into film studies by Etienne Souriau, who distinguished seven levels of filmic reality:[51]

1. Afilmic reality (the reality that exists independently of filmic reality)
2. Profilmic reality (the reality photographed by the camera)
3. Filmographic reality (the film as physical object, structured by techniques such as editing)
4. Screenic (or filmophanic) reality (the film as projected on a screen)
5. Diegetic reality (the fictional story world created by the film)
6. Spectatorial reality (the spectator's perception and comprehension of a film)
7. Creational reality (the filmmaker's intentions)

Souriau's discussion of the way these levels of reality relate to one another can be reformulated in terms of the container and in–out schemata. The in–out schema delimits the first boundary – between afilmic and profilmic reality. The afilmic exists outside the realm of the cinema, whereas the profilmic exists inside. But both these levels are then defined as existing outside the filmic text. This establishes a new boundary – between extra-textual and textual reality. Whereas the afilmic and profilmic are extratextual, the following three types of filmic reality are textual and are structured in relation to one another in terms of the container schema: The filmographic contains the screenic, and the screenic contains the diegesis. The final two levels of filmic reality are cognitive, referring to the spectator's comprehension of film and the film as conceived by the filmmaker.

In Souriau's terms, the frame exists on both the filmographic and screenic levels of filmic reality and serves as a container for the diegesis. But the relation between frame and diegesis in the cinema is complex. In painting and film, the frame serves as a boundary between what is seen and what remains unseen. Nonetheless, there is a fundamental difference between the function of the frame in painting and that in film. In painting, the frame acts as an absolute boundary; it unequivocally severs the bounded space from its surroundings. But in cinema, the frame is mobile. The boundary between bounded and unbounded space is equivocal. In filmic terms, there is an opposition between on-screen space and off-screen space. On-screen and off-screen space are themselves understood in terms of containment, since they contain the film's diegesis, or fictional story world. So the container schema operates at two levels of the film – the frame (which acts as a boundary between on-screen and off-screen space) and the diegesis (which acts as a boundary between fiction and non-fiction). Off-screen space has an unusual semiotic specificity, since it exists between the filmographic level and the screenic level of filmic reality. It is an invariant property of filmographic reality, but a variant property of screenic reality. In these terms, we can think of it as the potential, non-manifest stage of on-screen space.[52]

Off-screen space is therefore that part of the first container (the diegesis) that does not appear on screen and in frame (= the second container) at any one moment. The space of the auditorium, discussed earlier, can then be considered as the third and ultimate container. Although visual stimuli are contained within the frame and diegesis, sound is only contained by the third container, the auditorium. The auditorium is a container that contains the screen and frame. The frame is a container that contains the diegesis, the fictional story world (characters, settings, and actions). The auditorium, frame, and diegesis are container objects; what they contain are container substances – the auditorium contains the screen and frame (filmographic and screenic reality); the screen and frame contain the diegesis; the diegesis contains the fictional story world.

But the meaning of the container (or in-out) schema is equivocal when understood in terms of the cinema. 'In' can mean something hidden, unavailable, or unnoticed, the direct bodily meaning of 'in'. But in the cinema, it means the opposite – 'object x is in the image'. 'Out' also has two meanings – something previously hidden is brought to the forefront (again, the direct bodily meaning of 'out'), or the opposite, as in 'object x is out of the image'. This equivocation disappears only when we understand 'contained' in the cinema as a *transparent* container. So the cinema cannot be understood in direct analogy with the body, but in modified terms, since the body as an opaque container does not directly map onto the frame and diegesis, which are understood as transparent containers. It should now be quite evident that this transparent container is not a pre-existing entity (i.e., part of what is projected on screen), but is a default setting, a part of the spectator's competence, and it is precisely its status as a default setting that encourages the spectator to construct the film's diegesis mentally in her ongoing viewing of the film.

The frame can be comprehended in more specific ways as well. For example, whereas the framing of an objective (non-focalized) shot is comprehended as representing the vision of a non-diegetic narrator (unless of course you argue, like Bordwell, that non-diegetic filmic narrators do not exist), a subjective (or focalized) shot is comprehended as *embodied* – as representing the vision of a character existing in the diegesis. The frame in a subjective shot is therefore comprehended as being controlled within the diegesis, whereas the frame of an objective shot is perceived as disembodied and non-diegetic – but embodied in the film spectator's body. Of course, the subjective shot is also ultimately embodied in the film spectator, but that embodiment is duplicated in the film's diegesis.

Furthermore, what consequences does the mobile filmic frame have in terms of the body? Firstly, the fixed frame of painting reaffirms the fixed boundary of the body. But in the cinema, the frame is potentially mobile (its potentiality therefore defines it as a sub-code). But a mobile frame does not inherently signify anything. However, in conjunction with the narratological coding of the frame as subjective or objective, camera movement can be said to affect the body's absolute boundary between container and contained. If comprehended as subjective, the mobile frame represents the movement of a character within the diegesis (the frame is embodied in a mobile character). But when comprehended as objective, the mobile frame gives her vision a sense of transcendence. The enormous amount of writing devoted to the subjective (point of view, or focalized) shot attests the importance in perceiving a shot as objective or subjective.[53] A number of directors (such as Fritz Lang and Steven Spielberg) and genres (such as the horror film) play on the ambiguity of shots, in terms of whether they are subjective or objective, which determines the way we experience their films.[54]

The narrative film in itself is understood as a container, as is evident in everyday comments people make after seeing a film – "There was not much *in* the film" (the evaluation of a film employs terms of quantity – the more it contains, or the more that happens, the better); "I became immersed in (or absorbed *into*) the film" (here the spectator metaphorically views herself as an object drawn into the film as container); and so on. Heath employs the term 'suture' to describe the process that 'stitches' the spectator into an imaginary relation to the filmic image. By contrast, from a cognitive semantic perspective we can argue that the spectator's projection into the film is in fact the result of the container schema. This schema, directly motivated by the spectator's body, is metaphorically projected onto the film by the spectator in her ongoing construction of a mental representation of the film's diegesis as a coherent container. In Colin's example from *The Barefoot Contessa*, the spectator is involved in constructing the cabaret room as a container, and it is the successful completion of this activity that 'absorbs' the spectator into that space. Furthermore, the activity is facilitated by the frame, which necessarily excludes as well as includes. The frame's very act of exclusion prompts the spectator to begin mentally constructing the space of the room.

Lakoff's other schemata can also be applied to narrative films, with variable results. In terms of the part–whole schema, a narrative film is of course understood to be a whole made up of parts – shots and scenes. One of the main issues addressed by the structural linguistic–based film semiotics was to identify these parts by means of segmentation and classification. The part–whole schema is closely aligned to the link schema, since a collection of parts can only be perceived as a whole if the parts are linked coherently. Many of the techniques of continuity editing achieve this impression of coherence; they can therefore be understood in terms of the link schema. Some shots are central to a scene, such as the establishing shot, whereas others are less central, such as an analytical cut-in. A hierarchy of shot types could be established using the centre–periphery schema. Finally, narrative trajectories can be understood in terms of the source-path-goal schema, as Jan Simons has already demonstrated.[55]

This chapter only represents the beginnings of a cognitive semantic theory of film. When developed further, cognitive semantics will enable film scholars to overcome one of the primary limitations of both cognitive and psychoanalytic theories of spectatorship – their disembodied accounts of perception. Perception is not a process that only involves a relation between the eye and the mind (whether conscious or unconscious); more fundamentally, it involves the metaphorical projection of the body on screen and in frame.

CHAPTER THREE

Not What Is Seen through the Window but the Window Itself

Reflexivity, Enunciation, and Film

> In film, when enunciation is indicated in the utterance, it is not, or not essentially, by deictic imprints, but by *reflexive* constructions. ... The film talks to us about itself, about cinema, or about the position of the spectator. (Christian Metz)[1]

Throughout his career, Christian Metz was preoccupied – either directly or indirectly – with reflexivity in film. It is possible to identify three key moments: (1) his study of mirror constructions (*construction en abîme*) in Fellini's film *8½*; (2) a theory of enunciation based on Emile Benveniste's distinction between *histoire* (hi/story) and *discours* (discourse); and (3) his seminars of the late eighties, culminating in his book *L'Énonciation impersonnelle ou le site du film*.[2] In this chapter I will be investigating Metz's cognitive film semiotics (his theory of impersonal filmic enunciation), outlining the concepts it is based upon – particularly reflexivity, but also metalanguage and anaphora – and contrasting it with Francesco Casetti's cognitive film semiotics, a deictic theory of enunciation based on personal pronouns.[3] I shall attempt to articulate what I see to be the main difference between Casetti and Metz: Whereas Casetti models his theory on speech (on face-to-face conversation), Metz implicitly models his theory on writing. Metz rejected a pronoun-based theory of enunciation because, he argues, pronouns are not appropriate to describing the 'reality' of film. But Metz also rejected all deictic concepts (concepts that designate how film is oriented to its contexts of production and reception). I agree with Metz in rejecting Casetti's deictic theory of filmic enunciation (based on personal pronouns), but I do not agree with his rejecting deixis as a concept for describing the 'reality' of film and other audio-visual media. In contrast to Metz and Casetti, I suggest we understand 'deixis' as a broad cognitive concept, rather than a narrow linguistic one (which equates deixis with pronouns). Once we have freed deixis from its purely linguistic manifestation, we can use it to analyze how other audio-visual media are oriented to their contexts of production and reception. Toward the end of this chapter I shall reprieve the concept of deixis from Casetti's pronoun-based theory and from Metz's critique by demonstrating its value in describing the experience of watching television, as well as its usefulness in explaining the recent process of digital colorization of black and white films. Finally, I shall consider the implications of Metz's theory of impersonal enunciation for the textual analysis of films.

Reflexivity, Metalanguage, Anaphora

To identify a filmic text as reflexive is to suggest that it refers to itself – that is, foregrounds its own processes of production (its production as text). Here we see the explicit link between reflexivity and enunciation, because enunciation is precisely a process of production or mediation that transforms the underlying language system, *la langue*, into a text. This process of transformation leaves traces on the text, and it is the foregrounding of these traces that makes a text reflexive.

This connection between reflexivity and enunciation is completely absent from Metz's discussion of Fellini. However, in his paper "Histoire/Discours" this link becomes more apparent, although Metz uses the term 'exhibitionism' instead of 'reflexivity'. In its initial stages, the theory of filmic enunciation was dependent almost exclusively on Benveniste's distinction between enunciation and the utterance and, within the utterance, the distinction between *histoire* and *discours*. Metz transfers Benveniste's two forms of utterance to a psychoanalytical theory of vision: identifying exhibitionism with *discours* and voyeurism with *histoire*. The exhibitionist knows that she is being looked at and acknowledges the look of the spectator, just as *discours* acknowledges the speaker and hearer of the utterance, whereas the object of the voyeur's gaze does not know that she is being watched. The voyeur's look is secretive, concealed, like the marks of the speaker and hearer in *histoire*. Metz argued that classical narrative film is primarily voyeuristic – hence *histoire* – for it conceals its own discursive markers (here, the spectator's look), an activity other post-structural film theorists identified with film's ideological function and feminists with film's patriarchal function (for the look is traditionally conceived as mas-culine).

Benveniste's theory of enunciation therefore fits in quite well with the hierarchy dominating film semiotics. Enunciation denotes a process that mediates between the underlying non-perceptible system and the perceptible level. In fact, we could argue that enun-ciation denotes *the* major process mediating between the non-perceptible and the perceptible. The other concepts – suture, disa-vowal, patterns of repetition/alternation, and so on – arguably designate more specific processes of enunciation that mediate be-tween the non-perceptible and the perceptible.

Within the theory of filmic enunciation, all films were consid-ered to be constituted by marks of production and reception; the classical narrative film was then identified as a type of filmic text that attempts to conceal these marks (*discours* posing as *histoire*). Foregrounding the process of enunciation (making the text reflex-ive) breaks the illusion of continuity and reveals the codes that constitute this illusion. This is why the concept of enunciation ena-bled film theorists in the seventies to distinguish classical from modernist films – those that conceal their traces of enunciation, and those that emphasize these traces, respectively. Modernist films were then valorized because they implemented the same strategy as semiotics – that is, an investigation of the inner logic of filmic discourse.

Metz's theory of impersonal enunciation continues to discuss film in terms of reflexivity and enunciation, but this time with the concepts of metalanguage and anaphora, rather than Benveniste's distinction between *histoire* and *discours*. Metz's shift in terminology also marks a shift in his conception of filmic enunciation, since the first approach, based on Benveniste, finds a place of deictic terms, whereas the second, based on metalanguage and anaphora, rejects all reference to deixis.

As with most original theoretical texts, Metz's theory of imper-sonal filmic enunciation does not serve as an adequate introduction to its own concepts. Here I shall outline these concepts before mov-ing on to discuss Casetti's deictic theory of filmic enunciation.

For meaning to be determined, every language must have the capacity to refer to itself, as well as to extra-linguistic reality. By referring to itself, language becomes metalanguage, in opposition to object language, language referring to extra-linguistic reality.

Metalanguage is therefore one of the dominant ways in which language is used reflexively. In the following sentence (a constant source of irritation during my childhood)

(1) You should never say 'never'

The first use of 'never' belongs to the object (or first order) language, and the second to the meta- (or second order) language. Whereas signs functioning as object language are denotational, signs functioning as metalanguage are non-denotational, since they refer to language, not extra-linguistic reality. Metalanguage is not completely autonomous from the object language, since the same signs are used by both languages. The object language–metalanguage distinction is therefore a functional, rather than an ontological, distinction. Metalanguage cannot be reduced to a number of particular textual features, but refers to one potential function of *all* textual features. Metz transfers this insight to film: "Cinema does not have a closed list of enunciative signs, but it uses any sign . . . in an enunciative manner, so that the sign can be removed from the diegesis and immediately come back to it. The *construction* will have, for an instant, assumed an enunciative value."[4] This is one of the most radical and far-reaching conclusions of Metz's theory of impersonal enunciation, and I shall discuss it in more detail at the end of this chapter.

It is self-evident, then, that metalanguage is reflexive. For most linguists, reflexivity and metalanguage are essential attributes of natural language. But can these structures be located in cinematic language? Metz certainly believes so, and in his application of them to film, he emphasizes that they are forms of enunciation: "All figures of enunciation consist in metadiscursive folds of cinematic instances piled on top of each other."[5] Metz then gives an example: "In subjective framing, the gazing and at the same time showing character duplicates [that is, 'reflects'] both the spectator and the camera."[6]

Even back in 1964, in his paper "Cinéma: langue ou langage?" Metz implicitly acknowledged the reflexive (and therefore metadiscursive and enunciative) nature of filmic discourse. He gave the example of an image of a revolver, which, Metz tells us, does not signify "revolver" but "Here is a revolver." If the image simply signifies "revolver" it would be purely denotational (i.e., functioning as object language). But by signifying "*Here is* a revolver" the image also functions reflexively as metalanguage, since it acknowledges its own presentation of the revolver to a spectator. Furthermore, Metz conceives the reflexive dimension of the image deictically, since 'here' is a deictic term (more specifically, an adverb of place) that means 'proximate to the speaker (or spectator').

Anaphora designates another way in which language becomes reflexive. In fact, anaphora is a special form of metalanguage, since the referent of an anaphor is not an object or concept, but another linguistic sign. In the sentence

(2) John said that he is ill

'he' (the anaphor) is bound to 'John' (the antecedent). Moreover, the antecedent is the governing category, since it determines the meaning (or the reference) of the anaphor. Anaphora therefore expresses the reference back of one linguistic sign (the anaphor) to another linguistic sign (the antecedent).

The function of anaphora is to shorten and simplify sentences by avoiding the repetition of words within the same sentence. It also creates cohesion between sentences, as in the following example:

(3) John is ill. He will not be coming to work today

The substitution of 'he' for 'John' in the second sentence creates cohesion, since the anaphor in the second sentence is bound to the antecedent in the first sentence. Although Metz refers to anaphora on a number of occasions, he is concerned only with its reflexive and metadiscursive functions (its function as a mark of enunciation), not with its creation of economical, cohesive texts. Furthermore, he emphasizes the opposition between anaphora and deixis.

Anaphora therefore refers to a binding relation between two linguistic signs. It constitutes a purely internal (i.e., textual) relation, in which reference is made to information already contained in the utterance. But deixis signifies a relation between linguistic signs and their context. Deictic terms – including personal pronouns ('I', 'you'), demonstrative pronouns ('this', 'that', 'these', 'those'), and adverbs of time ('now', 'then') and place ('here', 'there') – refer directly to the circumstances of enunciation, primarily to the spatio-temporal position of speaker and hearer. In contrast, Saussure argued that meaning is generated from *la langue*, the underlying system consisting of pre-existing paradigmatic relations between linguistic signs. Saussure assumed that such signs are then simply manifest and organized in *la parole* (speech), the pragmatic dimension of language (*langage*) he excluded from his *Course in General Linguistics*. However, Benveniste in particular realized that a number of linguistic signs (deictic terms) only gain meaning when they are manifest in *la parole* (i.e., when they are used in concrete discursive situations). For example, the meaning of 'I' depends entirely on the person uttering it at that time. With the realization that some words gain meaning only when manifest, Benveniste understood that the relation between *la langue* and *la parole* needed investigating. He used the concept of enunciation to designate a process or activity that mediates between *la langue* (virtual/non-manifest system) and *la parole* (actual utterances). Enunciation is the process presupposed by the very existence of utterances.

By taking again the previous example

(4) John is ill. He will not be coming to work today

we note that, whereas 'he' is anaphoric, 'coming' and 'today' are deictic. The verb 'coming' in the phrase 'coming to work' suggests that the unidentified speaker is located in John's workplace (contrast it with 'He will not be *going* to work today'). Furthermore, the word 'today' is also deictic. Its meaning or reference is the day the speaker utters the word 'today'. When uttered on another day, its reference will obviously change. Its reference is therefore dependent on the circumstances of enunciation. Note, by contrast, that the anaphoric 'he' in the example will always refer to 'John', on whatever day the two sentences are uttered. Anaphors are not, therefore, dependent for their meaning on the circumstances of enunciation.

The shift within modern film theory from a film semiotics to post-structural theory closely shadowed the shift from structural linguistics to a theory of enunciation, particularly Benveniste's theory of deixis. Because deictic terms only gain their meaning when manifest, they obviously serve to bond or link the utterances to the speakers and hearers who produce and receive them. Indeed, language is not self-enclosed, but is oriented toward, or centred around, its users and their spatio-temporal context. Deictic words grammaticalize the reference points of production and reception within the utterance itself. The theory of deixis influenced the post-structural film theorists' concept of subject positioning, which was defined in terms of those reference points (especially the spectator's look) 'grammaticalized' (i.e., formally represented) in the film itself. Rather than conceptualized as a closed, autonomous entity, the filmic text in post-structural film theory is organized around an external reference point occupied by the spectator. This theory of meaning (which merely theorized the spectator as an absent centre point) was then enriched by Althusser's theory of interpellation (a discursive process that attempts to address each individual as a coherent and unified subject) and Lacan's linguistic re-reading of Freudian metapsychology.

The distinction between deixis and anaphora is crucial to understanding Metz's disputation with Francesco Casetti.

Francesco Casetti on 'Personal' Filmic Enunciation

Metz's theory of impersonal filmic enunciation is directly opposed to and formulated against Francesco Casetti's rigorous deictic theory of filmic enunciation, culminating in his book *Dentro lo sguardo* in 1986.[7] It may seem paradoxical, then, that Metz wrote the Preface to the French translation of *Dentro lo sguardo*.[8] However, when reading this Preface, we come to understand the influence Casetti had on Metz's own theory. Metz notes that, before he read the original Italian version of the book in 1986, the issue of filmic enunciation was running through his head, although his mind was unfocused. But after reading Casetti's book, Metz acknowledges that it persuaded him to work on a study of filmic enunciation.

Metz's debt to Casetti sounds very much like Kant's debt to Hume. Casetti certainly jolted Metz from his 'dogmatic slumbers', but his influence on Metz is indirect. Just as Kant did not become an empiricist, so Metz did not embrace Casetti's deictic theory of filmic enunciation. However, in his Preface Metz does not express his opposition to Casetti's deictic theory, but instead draws attention to a different opposition between his work and Casetti's: Whereas Casetti proposes a general conceptual framework to study filmic enunciation (supported by examples), Metz chose the "complementary direction" (as Metz puts it) to write about the numerous concrete forms of filmic enunciation.[9] Metz directly expressed his reservations about Casetti's deictic theory of filmic enunciation in a 1987 paper, "The Impersonal Enunciation, or the Site of Film" (quoted at the beginning of this chapter), which constitutes part 1 of *L'Énonciation impersonnelle*. Before I discuss Metz reservations, I shall outline the main argument of Casetti's work in the eighties.

In his essay "Looking for the Spectator," published in English in 1983 and constituting Chapter 1 of *Dentro lo sguardo*, Casetti charts the emergence of the spectator as a legitimate object of inquiry in film theory (rather than an unproblematic pregiven entity). When identified as an object of study (implicitly in the sixties, explicitly in the seventies), the spectator was conceptualized, Casetti notes, either as a *decoder* – "someone who can and must decipher a set of images and sounds" – or as an *interlocutor* – "someone to whom one can address propositions and from whom one may expect signs of intelligence."[10] The spectator as decoder is an implicit premise of film semiotics, because the spectator's role was marginalized in the production of filmic meaning (since films were conceived as autonomous entities).

Challenges to the conception of reader/spectator as decoder emerged from both literary and film theory; the most notable manifestations (listed by Casetti) were Barthes's theory of reading as rewriting, German theories of interpretation (based on phenomenology and hermeneutics), the implicit reader (Wolfgang Iser, M. Corti, Seymour Chatman), and the virtual reader (Jurij Lotman and Gerard Prince). Casetti also notes that in *Language and Cinema*, Metz admits, in his attempt to describe filmic codes and systems objectively, "a plurality of levels of reading, each of them submitted to a given 'principle of deciphering', and thus open to subjective choice and intervention."[11] Here, Casetti alludes to the tension in Metz's book between an empirically driven attempt to identify and classify filmic elements and the semiotic activity of modelling the underlying system that organizes these elements. Casetti then refers to Metz's well-known statement that the aim of film semiotics is "to understand how films are understood," a process that both Metz and Casetti characterize as a meta-reading of a film. (Of course, despite these allusions to spectators, only in *Psychoanalysis and Cinema* did the spectator take center stage in Metz's work.)

Placed center stage, the film spectator is conceived as an interlocutor (although to varying degrees by different film theorists). For Casetti, the most important aspects of conceptualizing the spectator as interlocutor are twofold: (1) "[the spectator] is in charge of weaving the threads of a fabric which is ultimately meant for him/her"; consequently, (2) the film is now conceived, not as an ordered and complete set of images and sounds that simply need to be attested (or decoded), but as a text, "an organism submitted to and influencing its context."[12] This definition of text implies that a film is not hermetically sealed from the outside, but is necessarily bonded to – or oriented toward – the outside world, and therefore is necessarily open and incomplete.[13]

It is at this point, or interface – between spectator-as-interlocutor and film-as-text – that Casetti makes his original intervention into the theory of filmic enunciation. To conceive spectators as interlocutors and films as texts strongly implies the film's necessary orientation toward a spectator:

At every moment, the film indicates a point where it can anchor its own moves and find a response; it directs its looks and voices, beyond the limits of the scene, toward someone who presumably (or rather, pretendingly) has to collect them and to answer back. Briefly stated, the film *offers itself* for viewing – instituting its own destination as a goal to be reached, or a backboard on which to bounce again.[14]

In response to a film offering itself for viewing, the spectator "*commits* him/herself to viewing: s/he responds to the availability of the world-on-the-screen by taking his/her own responsibility in response to the propositions of a destination by the film."[15]

Finally, Casetti briefly indicates that pragmatics is able to act as a framework for his study, since it also theorizes the relation between text and its contexts (particularly its context of reception)[16] and enables the film theorist to ask about "how the film entertains its interlocutor, how it founds his/her presence, organizes his/her action, etc, in a word, how the film says 'you'."[17]

It is to this question that Casetti addresses himself in his subsequent essay "Face to Face"[18] (published in 1983 and containing the central hypotheses of *Dentro lo sguardo*). Casetti points out that film is not a self-enclosed work but a text that opens "in itself a space ready to receive whomever it is addressed to."[19] The essay is dedicated to the task of describing this space in detail, employing deictic categories of person.

Casetti begins by considering the openings of two films – *Riso Amaro* (Guiseppe de Santis, 1949) and *The King of Marvin Gardens* (Bob Rafelson, 1972). Both begin with a character looking directly at the camera, a technique that Casetti characterizes as a form of direct interpellation that transgresses a well-known interdiction and functions metadiscursively by drawing attention to the process of filmic enunciation. Casetti then evokes the following series of oppositions to distinguish films (or segments of films) that draw attention to their enunciation and films that attempt to disguise their enunciation: discourse/story, commentary/narrative, and enunciative utterance/utterative text, respectively. He holds to the principle that "there are permanent marks [of enunciation] accompanying the filmic text all along its development," in which the addressee represents one of these marks.[20] A character's look at the camera is a textual mark that affirms the presence of an addressee/spectator. In Casetti's words, this is one filmic technique that says 'you'.

Through an analysis of the opening sequence of *The Kid from Spain* (Leo McCarey, 1932), Casetti develops, using the deictic categories 'I', 'you', and 'he', his typology of shot types, a typology that goes some way toward describing the space that opens out a film (or a scene) to each spectator (or her look):

The relation between a look and a scene allows us to appraise at the same time the enunciator, addressee and the discourse they control, that is to say, a group of three elements that correspond to, respectively, the gesture of actualization thanks to which one sees, the gesture of destination that gives itself to be seen, and the thing (or the character) that is seen. In fact, if we want to establish indicative identities, we have an *I*, a *you* and a *he* (character or thing).[21]

For Casetti, this system of three gestures (or elements) is obligatory in all films (it constitutes the film's conditions of possibility). Although these elements are invariant, Casetti allows for a shift in emphasis on one at the expense of the others; indeed, his typology is based on the hierarchical re-configuration of these elements.

The first type of shot Casetti identifies is based on a fundamental equilibrium between the elements. Attention is drawn neither to the enunciator ('I') nor to the addressee ('you'), but only to the film itself (the utterance, or 'he').

Opposite a *he* that shows itself for what it is, there is an *I* and a *you* that are present but which do not make their presence explicit. In particular, the addressee must assume the position of a witness: he is the one who is led to look, and therefore who is permitted to look, but without this mandate being made explicit and without this task (of looking) intervening in the events.[22]

This is the "objective shot," or film as *histoire*/narrative/utterative text. What Casetti means here is that, as with all discourse, the objective filmic shot presupposes an enunicator – or an 'I' ("the gesture of actualization") – and an addressee – or a 'you' ("the gesture of destination"), although attention is not drawn to these two 'gestures'. According to Casetti, their presence is not, therefore, explicit, but implicit, in the objective shot. We can take this to mean that these two gestures are understood by the spectator to be present, even though they are not marked in the shot. Examples of the object shot are numerous, and Casetti refers to a moment in *The Kid from Spain* when a group of girls talk to one another without acknowledging the look of the camera.

The second type of shot is interpellation, which ruptures the equilibrium apparent in the first type, since both the enunciator's ('I') and the addressee's ('you') presence become explicit in the utterance (although unequally). A character's look at the addressee is a seminal case of interpellation. Casetti formally defines interpellation as follows:

An *I* (who looks and sees) coincides with a *he* (who is seen but at the same time looks at he [the spectator] who is led to look), whereas a *you* (who is meant to be looked at and is looked at, but is not seen) enters in the game without assuming any precise form. The enunciator is represented in a character, who depends on a question of action (the act of looking) and a question of framing (reaching the spectator), effecting a slippage from the level of enunciation to the level of the utterance.[23]

What Casetti means in effect is that the enunciator ('I') enters the film through the intermediary of a character's look ('he'), which is directly addressed to the spectator ('you').

The third type of shot is the subjective shot, consisting of two moments – a character's act of looking and the addressee's being shown what the character is looking at (these two moments can be shown in one, two, or three shots). Casetti conceives these two moments as a series that goes from "You and I see him" to "You and he see what I show you."[24] Here, the character ('he') and addressee ('you') become prominent.

Finally, Casetti calls the fourth type of shot an "unreal objective shot," referring to unusual camera angles. Casetti gives the example of those shots found in Busby Berkeley musicals in which the camera is placed perpendicular to the horizon – when it is pointing downwards on a group of dancers who form an abstract pattern (an example of which is found in *The Kid from Spain*). According to Casetti, the deictic formula is " 'as if *you* were *I*': the addressee renounces his own competence in order to slide into the other. He confines himself to a pure faculty of seeing, to a look without a determinate place."[25] This type of shot is characterized by the inability to attribute it to a character, and by the absence of enunciator and addressee (only the camera's look is present).

How do these four canonical shots characterize their addressee? Casetti argues the following:

The addressee [assumes] respectively the posture of the witness (a confirmed *you* opposite a confirmed *I*: the "objective shot"), the spectator set aside (a *you* installed opposite an *I* combined with a *he*: interpellation), the character (a *you* combined with a *he* opposite a confirmed *I*: the "subjective shot") and the camera (a *you* combined with an *I*: the "unreal objective shot").[26]

In other words, we have the following schema:

Shot	*Addressee*
Objective	Witness
Interpellation	Spectator set aside
Subjective	Identification with character
Unreal objective	Identification with camera

This is Casetti's basic framework for describing the film's orientation toward the spectator-as-interlocutor.

Figure 4 shows how Casetti complexifies Metz's application to film of Benveniste's distinction *histoire/discours*. Although shot types 1 and 4 (like 2 and 3) use personal pronouns, only the third person pronoun, which is an anaphoric term, not a deictic term (and it is anaphoric because it is an indirect form of address, unlike the first and second persons), is visible. This is why 1 and 4 conform to *histoire*, not *discours*.

Christian Metz on Impersonal Filmic Enunciation

One of the main arguments in Metz's last published book is that filmic enunciation is resolutely non-deictic, and therefore does not require pronouns to describe it: "Personal pronouns can only lead toward *a deictic conception of enunciation in cinema*, which in my

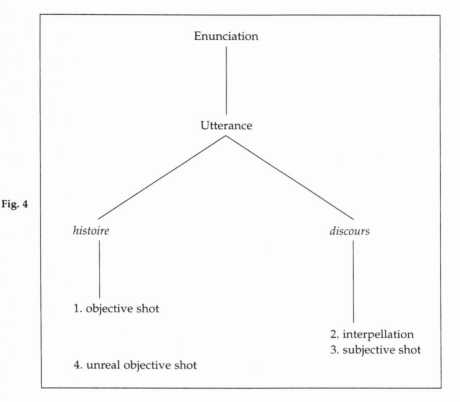

Fig. 4

opinion is not suitable to the realities of film.''[27] As we have seen, Metz argues that the realities of film are conducive to anaphora (in which one piece of text refers to another piece of text) but not deixis (in which a piece of text must refer to its context of enunciation for its meaning). For Metz, the reality of oral discourse allows for a strong distinction between deixis and anaphora; written language allows for a weak distinction; whereas in filmic discourse, there is only anaphora.

Although the linguistic theory of enunciation began as a theory of personal pronouns, Metz resolutely rejects all notions that the link between enunciation and pronouns is determinate. Casetti, however, identifies enunciation with pronouns. Metz lists three main risks in doing this: (1) anthropomorphism, (2) artificial use of linguistic concepts, and (3) transformation of enunciation into a dialogue (involving 'real', extra-textual relationships).[28] Metz's main criticism of Casetti revolves around point 2. Before discussing this point, I shall briefly go over points 1 and 3.

First of all, to prevent anthropomorphism, Metz prefers to speak of source and target of enunciation, rather than enunciator and addressee.[29] Furthermore, he argues that these terms designate nothing more than parts of texts, or orientations. What he means by this latter term is that the source is the text as "seen from its origin to its end" (for Casetti, the film in the process of being made); the target is the same text, but this time seen from its end point "being undone and freed in imagination"[30] (for Casetti, the film in the moment it gives itself to be seen).

With reference to point 3, Metz notes that, whereas dialogue is an empirical activity, involving actual interlocutors, enunciation is a purely textual phenomenon:

It is of no use to pretend with all the required discretion that knowledge of the enunciator and the addressee would give us at least probabilities or general frames to understand the author's intentions and the spectator's reactions. For these forecasts are so general that no empirical analysis would take them into account and they could prove to be wrong for any given spectator, even if they express a partial tendency common to every-one. The reason why is that you deal with two heterogeneous orders of reality, a text (that is, I repeat, a thing) and persons.[31]

To prevent misunderstanding, Metz adds the following rejoinder: "I don't pretend here that enunciative configurations are deprived of any influence on the observable behaviour of the spectators (this hypothesis is as improbable as that of its unmistakable determination by the film)."[32]

We now come to what Metz characterizes as Casetti's artificial use of linguistic concepts. In particular, Metz questions Casetti's specific use of personal pronouns to describe aspects of filmic reality before rejecting outright a deictic theory of filmic enunciation. First of all, he questions Casetti's identification of the enunciator with the 'I' – that is, the subject of the utterance (the filmmaker); Metz argues that it is more plausible to identify the subject with the spectator, as film theorists in the seventies had. Moreover, Metz rejects the symmetry posited by Casetti's deictic formulas, which suggest that enunciator and addressee have equal status, that both are roles to be invested with bodies. But Metz argues that this

symmetry is merely a symptom of the use of the first two persons
of natural language (of Casetti's speech model of film):

Where the enunciator is concerned, there is no body. And since it is true
that roles (or their equivalents in another theoretical frame) call for an
incarnation – the nature of this call still remains enigmatic – the "enunciator" is incarnated in the only available body, the body of the text, that is, a
thing, which will never be an I, which is not in charge of any exchange
with some You, but which is a source of images and sounds, and nothing
else. *The film is the enunciator*, the film as source, acting as such, *oriented* as
such, the film as activity. Casetti's idea, that a body would be needed for
the enunciator as well as for the addressee, is inspired by the first two
persons of the verb in languages.[33]

Metz comes close to Bordwell's rejection of the narrator (see Chapter 2), but he does not, of course, reject linguistics, as Bordwell
does. Instead, Metz simply repeats that film theorists should not
draw analogies between film and natural language. This is evident
when he challenges Casetti's identification of film/character with
the third person pronoun. Metz finds this paradoxical because, in
Benveniste's famous definition, the third person is the absent non-
person, in opposition to the first ('I') and second ('you') persons,
who are present. But in the cinema, "the film, far from being an
absent instance stuck between two present ones, would resemble
rather a present instance stuck between two absent ones, the author,
who disappears after the fabrication, and the spectator, who is
present but does not manifest his presence in any respect."[34]

Metz is equally critical of Casetti's attribution of the verbs 'to
look/watch' and 'to see' to the 'I' (the filmmaker): "[The filmmaker]
does not watch, he has watched (which is still not entirely accurate:
he has filmed, and, therefore, watched; the 'utterer' [émetteur] does
not watch his film; he makes it)."[35] What Metz clearly means is that
the filmmaker, when watching his film, becomes its addressee (a
'you' in Casetti's terms). In this sense, then, the 'I' does not watch:
"From the source, nothing either watches or sees, the source produces, expands, *shows*."[36]

Finally, Metz attempts to demonstrate the arbitrariness of Casetti's deictic formulas. He argues this point by using the 'orienta-
tional' approach he developed to combat the anthropomorphism of
a deictic theory. Metz simply reorients himself to the opposite side
of the filmic text. For example, this is how he discusses Casetti's
formulation of the subjective shot:

According to Casetti, the enunciator plays a silent role and the addressee on the contrary is very much highlighted, since he is 'syncretized' with a concrete character, through whose very eyes we see what we see, and who is therefore, like the addressee, a watcher. . . . That is beyond doubt. But it is also true, if you turn over the text, that the enunciator regains his importance, in that the source is 'figurativized' in a character who is not only a watcher (as the spectator), but is also someone who shows, like the filmmaker who stands behind him. This character has one eye in front and one eye in back, he receives rays from both sides, and the image can be perceived in two different ways, as in some drawings in which form and background can be inverted.[37]

Metz is then at pains to emphasize that the reversibility he speaks of is totally different to the reversibility of interlocutors in a dialogue – a reversibility made possible by personal pronouns! In fact Metz is quite right; he points out that, in a dialogue, the deictic signifiers change referents, constituting the actual movement/reversibility of oral exchange, whereas the reversibility he speaks of is an analyst simply changing his theoretical viewpoint.

Metz concedes that not all figures of enunciation can be reversed, since some are precisely imprinted in a film (this means then, that the subjective shot, which Metz did reverse, is not precisely imprinted on a film). In Casetti's formulas, Metz mentions that the unreal objective shot cannot be reversed (Metz refers not to the Busby Berkeley examples, but to the systematic use of low angles in the films of Orson Welles).

We can now begin to articulate the fundamental difference between Casetti and Metz. Whereas Casetti models film on the immediacy and symmetry between filmic enunciator and addressee, as in a dialogue, Metz argues for the mediate and non-symmetrical nature of the relation between filmic enunciator and addressee – as in writing. This relation is non-symmetrical because one of the functions of writing is to dispense with the presence of the enunciator (or allow a spatio-temporal displacement between the enunciator and her utterance). Similarly, Metz dispenses with the filmic enunciator because of the way he conceives the realities of the filmic medium – it resembles the recording activity and permanence of writing rather than the immediacy and impermanence of speech. More specifically, Metz conceives film as a particular type of writing, namely, *histoire*, which Benveniste defined by its absence of deictic markers.

A consequence of the reality of the filmic medium (its reality as *histoire*) is that it records unique spatio-temporal events (and therefore no longer makes the perception of these events unique). Yet Metz does not explore this aspect of film – or indeed of television. More generally, Metz does not explore the relation between the space and time depicted in a film/on TV and the space and time of the film/TV viewer's situation. But this is crucial in the comprehension of both film and TV images and represents a deictic bond between the spectator/viewer and the image, a bond Metz refuses to acknowledge. By rejecting Casetti's use of deictics, Metz has rejected all forms of deictic orientation of images toward their contexts of production and reception. It is to this limitation in Metz's theory that I shall now turn.

Deixis, Television, and Digital Colorization

According to Metz, film does not orient itself in relation to the spatio-temporal circumstances of its production and reception, but can only orient itself in relation to its own internal spatio-temporal relationships – relations between its shots and between its autonomous segments: "The film is able to express space and time relationships of some kind, but only anaphorically, within the film itself, between its different parts, and not between the film and someone or something else."[38] This is why, for Metz, "Enunciation is the semiological act by which some parts of a text talk to us about this text as an act. However, resorting to the complicated and quasi-inimitable mechanism of the deixis is not a necessity."[39] Instead, he argues that "cinematic enunciation is always enunciation on the film. Reflexive, rather than deictic, it does not give us any information about the outside of the text, but about a text that carries in itself its source and its destination."[40]

Metz's theory of impersonal enunciation only functions within a specific (or narrowly defined) framework. I have mentioned that Metz aligns film to writing (or to *histoire*) rather than speech. Because of the absence in *histoire* of deixis and its select use of a limited set of tenses (the aorist, imperfect, and pluperfect),[41] *histoire* represents events that are not spatio-temporally related to the context of the writer/enunciator. The events narrated by the historian are not related, by deixis and/or by tense, to the present (to the context of utterance).

On the other hand, *discours* is related to its context of utterance. Benveniste argues this by referring to the perfect tense:

The perfect creates a living connection between the past event and the present in which its evocation takes place. It is the tense for the one who relates the facts as a witness, as a participant; it is thus the tense that will be chosen by whoever wishes to make the reported event ring vividly in our ears and to link it to the present. Like the present [tense], the perfect belongs to the linguistic system of discourse, for the temporal location of the perfect is the moment of the discourse while the location of the aorist [a tense exclusive to *histoire*] is the moment of the event.[42]

In rejecting the presence of deixis in film, Metz limits his discussion of filmic enunciation to the articulation of space and time within narrative fiction films (as he did when formulating his *grande syntagmatique* in the sixties). He argues that spectators do not need to know anything about the circumstances of enunciation to comprehend a film's internal spatio-temporal relations. It is indeed the case that each fiction film does not require any deictic relation to the space and time of its production and reception to comprehend its internal spatio-temporal relations, since the film's own space-time relations constitute an imaginary elsewhere and remain an imaginary elsewhere each time and place in which it is projected. Yet there is more to understanding a narrative film than simply comprehending the internal spatio-temporal relations of its diegesis. I propose to steer a course between Casetti's personal pronoun theory of filmic enunciation and Metz's theory of impersonal enunciation based only on anaphora. In other words, we need to supplement Metz's theory with deictic terms – as long as we understand deixis to be a general cognitive category, not a narrow linguistic one. In the 1930s Karl Bühler used the term 'deixis' in this broad sense to develop what he called a situation model of action, which studies "the meaningful behaviour of the living being."[43] More specifically, Bühler used the term deixis to study the systems of orientation that enable an individual to orient herself in relation to her environment. Bühler gives the example of an individual attempting to orient herself in a new city. Each individual's mode of orientation is not limited to deixis in speech, but also includes the physical act of pointing (ocular deixis, or pointing that takes place within a common space of actual perception) and what Bühler calls imagination-oriented deixis (orientation in fictional spaces). Of course, these various types of deixis work in conjunction with one another to give the individual a detailed mental map of her environment. Interestingly, in outlining the way ocular deixis interacts with linguistic deixis, Bühler emphasizes the role of the individual's body: "When [a] person uses words like *in front–behind, right–left, above–below* [a] fact becomes apparent, namely the fact that he *senses his body*, too, in *relation* to his optical orientation, and employs it to point. His (conscious, experienced) *tactile body image* has a position in relation to visual space."[44] Bühler anticipates the work of George Lakoff and other cognitive semanticists by fifty years.

I want to use this broad understanding of deixis to begin explaining how spectators comprehend documentary films, home movies, and TV news programs. Whereas in narrative fiction films the internal spatio-temporal relations are specific, the film's relation to the extra-filmic space-time of its production and reception is nonspecific, as we have already seen. But in the comprehension of home movies and TV news, both the internal *and* external spatio-temporal relations are specific (or perhaps we should say, they need to be specific for comprehension to take place). That is, the relation between the space and time of an event depicted in the TV news (for example) and the space and time of the TV spectator must be specified, since news images obviously gain their meaning from the spatio-temporal context in which they are manifest (they are deictically bound to their context of reception).

This can be understood more clearly by referring to Daniel Dayan and Elihu Katz's work on the televisation of live events.[45] They begin by making a distinction between spectacle, ceremony, and festival. Whereas spectacle involves a minimum level of interaction between performers and audience, festival involves a strong interaction (with ceremony falling somewhere in between). In this sense, both film and TV are spectacles because they minimize interaction between performers and audience through spatio-temporal displacement. In festivals, on the other hand, there is minimal displacement because the audience becomes part of the event (they are as much part of the event as the performers); in other words, it is difficult to separate audience from performers. Ceremonies depend on a reaction from the audience (shouting, applause, etc.), although this is their only level of interaction.

Katz and Dayan then ask, What happens when ceremonies are televised and broadcast live? Their main argument is that television enables spectators to attend the whole of the event as it unfolds and maintains a sense of continuity and immediacy between spectators and performers. If recorded, events become spectacles, but if they are broadcast live, the activity of watching them on TV allows the audience to feel a part of (rather than apart from) the event. There is therefore a determinate link between the TV image and the audience, since the spatio-temporal relations between the TV audience and the televised event become specific: The audience is oriented toward the event as it unfolds in real time and in continuous space. Under these conditions, I would characterize the link between the event and the TV audience as deictic (more specifically, ocular deixis), since the broadcast gains its meaning (as deictic terms do) by maintaining a direct and continuous link between an event and its context of reception – its audience. In live broadcasts, the whole of the TV apparatus functions deictically.

It appears, then, that it is the recording aspect of film and TV that disqualifies us from defining them in terms of deixis. This is what Metz argues when he aligns film with writing. In opposition to Metz, I argue that the act of recording, like other means of production, also creates deictic links between the image and its context (although in this instance, the image creates a link with its context of production, not reception). It is quite reasonable to argue that all film and TV images are embodied with their technological mode of production, which binds each to an historical space and time. This phenomenon is particularly accentuated in early films, by innovations in film technology (black and white emulsions, Technicolor, colorization), camera technology (such as the development of wide screen), and projection technology (Dolby stereo, etc.). Indeed, what does the recent practice of digital colorization of black and white films signify except a disparity between the reception of films by their contemporary audience and the purported intolerance of today's audiences, who perceive black and white images as 'dated'? The so-called need for colorization is an indication that the black and white nature of filmic images is a mark of enunciation, a mark of the film's historical context of production. For today's audiences, brought up on color images, the black and white nature of film images becomes reflexive or metalinguistic (is rendered reflexive by historical time). Digital colorization seems to me, then, to be a 'mechanism of disguise' that attempts to conceal a form of filmic enunciation (here, black and whiteness). Paradoxically, however, the black and white nature of these films is accentuated through its very effacement.

The Impossibility of Textual Analysis?

Metz's theory of impersonal filmic enunciation can be taken in another direction. I shall return to his notion that marks of enunciation only have a functional, rather than an ontological, status in the filmic text, then briefly mention the work of a number of American film scholars who have independently adopted a functional approach.

In the previous section I highlighted the negative side of Metz's rejection of deixis. But this rejection has a positive side – it discards the empiricist claim that marks of enunciation are inherent in a text and simply need to be identified and read off the film's surface. According to deictic theories of filmic enunciation, a film's formal configuration (its framing, inherent perspectival system, *mise-en-scène*, and so on), 'gang up' to designate a place or position for each spectator who watches the film. But Metz's work on impersonal filmic enunciation brings into question the power of these formal configurations, which are treated as if they are empirical objects that automatically and unfailingly position each spectator. A theory of enunciation can no longer point to a particular textual figure and argue that it constitutes a mark of enunciation, that it positions every spectator or determines her psychic disposition toward the text.

This theoretical position, in which texts do not (or cannot) determine their own reading, has been developed within both deconstruction and reception studies. For Paul de Man, the rhetorical structure of a text will in the end prevent the analyst from applying to that text a preconceived interpretive method or reducing it to a prior set of general theoretical assumptions. Each textual reading is also a misreading, because it focuses only on those elements of the text that conform to these general theoretical assumptions at the expense of discrepant elements, a residue of indetermination that resists generalization. Although reception studies also posits that texts are inherently indeterminate, its advocates argue that textual meaning is temporarily fixed in different ways by different interpretive communities. Whereas reception studies focuses on indeterminate texts as they are consumed and interpreted by various communities, deconstruction focuses on textual indeterminacy from a vantage point that is not in itself interpretive.

In contrast, the primary aim of structural-based textual analysis was to replicate the structure of a text in a theoretical language, to model a structure not immediately manifest to perception because only the effects of structures are perceived, rather than the structures themselves. But this process of replication in fact diminishes the text, reduces it to a preconceived structural grammar. The idea of a progressive filmic text, first advocated by the editors of *Cahiers du cinéma* in the late sixties, acknowledges discrepant details in a text – details that cannot be reduced to a preconceived grammar. This reading strategy codifies these discrepancies as contradictory, progressive moments that are inscribed on (and can simply be read off) a film's surface.

Metz's comments on the functional status of marks of enunciation challenge the assumptions of structuralism, the progressive text, as well as reception studies. Metz questions the notion that a text can be labelled as *inherently* feminist, progressive, reactionary – or even reflexive (although Metz did not draw out these consequences from his comments). It seems to me that Metz's theory of impersonal filmic enunciation is an enunciative theory implicitly based on the premises of deconstruction – most notably, the inherent indeterminacy of texts. This is evident in his refusal to consider relations between the text and its extra-textual contexts of production and reception, as well as in the way he reverses some of Casetti's deictic formulas, thereby rendering them indeterminate. Although I concur with Metz's deconstruction of Casetti, I would not go so far as to deconstruct all attempts to relate a filmic text to extra-textual reality.

Metz's deconstructive position foreshadows recent work by American film theorists, including Judith Halberstam, David Rodowick, and Tom Conley. All three authors in their own way approach the question, How does textual analysis progress, after realizing that its cherished filmic text is indeterminate? In a chapter on *The Silence of the Lambs* (Jonathan Demme, 1991), Halberstam argues that "we are at a peculiar time in history, a time when it is becoming impossible to tell the difference between prejudice and its representations, between, then, homophobia and the representations of homophobia."[46] In relation to Demme's film, Halberstam avoids the temptation to advance generalized claims that seek to reduce the film to some preconceived interpretive method:

I resist here the temptation to submit Demme's film to a straightforward feminist analysis that would identify the danger of showing mass audiences an aestheticized version of the serial killing of women. I resist the temptation to brand the film as homophobic because gender confusion becomes the guilty secret of the mad man in the basement. I resist, indeed, the readings that want to puncture the surface and enter the misogynist and homophobic unconscious of Buffalo Bill, Hannibal the Cannibal and Clarice Starling. This film, indeed, demands that we stay at the surface and look for places where the surface stretches too thin.[47]

However, Halberstam presents a peculiar mix of reception studies, deconstruction, and the theory of intentionality. The preceding excerpt is structured by a rhetoric that, firstly, asserts the different readings of the film by various communities (gay men, heterosexual feminists, and lesbians) and, secondly, at the same time resists these readings by declaring the inherent indeterminacy of the film itself. These two strategies can be seen to complement one another, for both deconstruction and reception studies are based on the concept of textual indeterminacy. But Halberstam then undermines this emphasis on indeterminacy by ascribing intentionality to the film: "*The film indeed demands* that we stay at the surface" (my emphasis). The fallacy of ascribing agency to a text is compounded by the logical conflict between the theory of intentionality (which fixes textual meaning in advance) and the deconstructive and reception studies' emphasis on textual indeterminacy. Halberstam is undecidable when it comes to choosing between these incompatible theories of textuality.

Both Rodowick and Conley combine deconstruction and reception studies with textuality in a more positive and 'decidable' manner than Halberstam does. They advocate a practice of politically creative re-reading of films, one that does not passively reproduce the dominant values indeterminately perpetuated through filmic texts. Rodowick argues for textual criticism that "must be understood not as repeating what a text means, but as presenting the opportunity to construct positions from which it can always be read and understood in new and unforeseen ways."[48] For Rodowick, then, critical reading becomes an act of creative intervention in which the reading encounters the text in a relation of difference, not identity.

Similarly, Conley develops a creatively political practice of reading by analyzing the presence of alphabetical writing in narrative films. Following Derrida's critique of the subservience of writing to speech and his subsequent emphasis on the alterity of these two channels of discourse, Conley places the image on the side of spoken language against written language and in so doing posits an essential difference between writing and filmic image. Conley's main aim is to trace the movement of difference between writing (film titles, shop and road signs, etc.) and the film images in which it appears. He notes that these two channels of discourse result in

an activity – a pleasure – of analysis allowing spectators to rewrite and rework discourses of film into configurations that need not be determined by what is immediately before the eyes. Reworking of this order can lead, it is hoped, to creatively political acts of viewing. In this way, the literal aspect of film writing can engage methods of viewing that need not depend entirely upon narrative analysis.[49]

Conley wants to articulate and politicize the personal fantasies of each spectator when she sub-consciously experiences the marginal (non-narrative) details within the filmic image. Conley's and Rodowick's answers to the question, How does textual analysis progress, after realizing that its cherished filmic text is indeterminate?, are important because they offer a way out of the impasse expressed by Halberstam and, more generally, refute commentators who reduce deconstruction to a theory focusing on the mere play of signifiers.

Yet it is unfortunate that Metz did not develop this second – functional – dimension of his work; unfortunate because it can be taken in the direction independently developed by Rodowick and Conley. Metz's innovation therefore seems to be primarily negative – a critique of Casetti's analogies between film and natural language. To this extent, Metz has returned to and repeated the negative tone of his first paper "Film: langue ou langage?" in which he rejected a comparison between film and *la langue*. In *L'Énonciation impersonnelle*, Metz also committed himself to a more reflexive style of writing, a style he gradually developed since the mid-seventies. It would take another chapter to discuss this issue in Metz's works; I shall simply note here that, at the beginning and ending of "The Imaginary Signifier," Metz writes about the very activity of theorizing about the cinema and highlights its paradoxes.[50] And in "The

Impersonal Enunciation" he combines his reflexive style with a more personal style of writing (the paper and the book it is part of serve to acknowledge the support his friends and colleagues have given him over the years). It is fitting, then, that toward the end of the paper Metz argues that the validity of research into the cinema is, in the end, dependent on the personal qualities of the individual researcher: "If you assume that the analyst has the necessary training (knowledge, method), the whole value of his work depends on his personal qualities, since he is at the same time the scholar, and (together with the film), the very terrain of the research."[51]

The question posed previously – How does textual analysis progress, after realizing that its cherished filmic text is indeterminate? – has not been tackled only by American film scholars. The cognitive film semiotician Roger Odin has made the truism that texts cannot determine their own reading a fundamental premise of his semio-pragmatic approach to film. Odin's work is analyzed in the following chapter.

CHAPTER FOUR

The Institutional Context

A Semio-pragmatic Approach to Fiction and Documentary Film

I do not think, I no longer think today, that it is interesting to pose the problems of the relations between the immanentist paradigm and the pragmatic paradigm in terms of exclusion or conflict... The consequence of these reflections is that to understand how film is understood necessitates the inclusion of the immanent and pragmatic approaches in the same theoretical framework. As its name indicates, semio-pragmatic attempts to articulate these two paradigms. (Roger Odin)[1]

The most promising [definitions of pragmatics] are the definitions that equate pragmatics with 'meaning minus semantics', or with a theory of language understanding that takes context into account, in order to complement the contribution that semantics makes to meaning. (Stephen Levinson)[2]

In conjunction with that of the other cognitive film semioticians I have already discussed in this book, Roger Odin's semio-pragmatic film theory is preoccupied with researching the film spectator's competence, the tacit knowledge that constitutes each spectator's psychic disposition (or mode of attention) when engaged in the activity of watching a film. Odin regards filmic competence as predominantly pragmatic, with the result that meaning is determined, not by the internal, semantic constraints of *la langue,* or contingent grammatical rules, or by deictic markers, but by a multitude of external constraints.

Odin calls these external constraints 'institutions', a concept central not only to pragmatics, but also to sociology and anthropology. For Bronislaw Malinowski, an institution

implies an agreement on a set of traditional values for which human beings come together. It also implies that these human beings stand in definite relation to one another and to a specific physical part of their environment, natural and artificial. Under the charter of their purpose or traditional

mandate, obeying the specific norms of their association, working through
the material apparatus which they manipulate, human beings act together
and thus satisfy some of their desires, while also producing an impression
on their environment.[3]

One fundamental component of Odin's semio-pragmatics is that
the institution-spectator-film interaction is not predetermined and
failsafe. The ontology of a film is not automatically fixed in advance, but is determined through the process of watching (or reading) a film. This means that no film can be defined as inherently
fictional, documentary, or avant-garde. Odin shows that such
'modes' of film are not given in advance, but are the effect, or end
result, of a series of 'operations'. A crucial feature of Odin's work
is to delineate the various filmic modes and operations.

Another aspect of semio-pragmatics is that the modes of film
are not seen to be mutually exclusive categories, but share a number of operations. Odin argues that only one operation (fictivization) separates the fiction and documentary modes of filmmaking.
To this extent, Odin's work reinforces recent debates concerning
the close relation between fiction and documentary films.[4] Later I
shall outline all the primary 'modes' Odin identifies, and the 'operations' they share and discuss three particular modes of filmmaking central to Odin's work – the documentary, home movie, and
'dynamic' modes. But first, I shall outline the foundations of Odin's
film theory, which is based on a three-way relation between semiotics, pragmatics, and cognitivism.

Meaning, Context, and the Mind

Pragmatics is not a unified, homogeneous discipline, but is multiple
and diverse. Francesco Casetti identifies four dominant schools of
pragmatics:[5] (1) empirical pragmatics (based on psycho- and socio-
linguistics), (2) transcendental (or universal) pragmatics (as formulated by Jürgen Habermas), (3) illocutionary pragmatics (based
on speech act theory), and (4) enunciative pragmatics (theories of
enunciation, which I have discussed in Chapter 3). Whereas empirical pragmatics studies many of the contingent, ad hoc influences
on speech (class, gender, geographical location), and universal
pragmatics studies an 'ideal speech situation', illocutionary and
enunciative pragmatics study linguistic competence, delimiting its
domain of research to specific dimensions of language (such as
pronouns, which encode context in language form), as well as in-

trospective (or cognitive) dimensions of language (for example, inference generation). Despite their diversity, all schools of pragmatics propose that language meaning is not fixed in advance. Pragmatists study the relation between language and context, and all agree that understanding language is not simply a matter of knowing the meaning of words and the grammatical relations between them, but depends on knowing how to use language in various contexts.

Odin's film theory possesses a cognitive dimension and a pragmatic dimension, which firmly align it to a recent paradigm within linguistics, one Casetti does not identify – what Melina Sinclair calls cognitive (or mentalist) pragmatics.[6] She identifies this position in the work of a number of prominent linguists, including Jan Nuyts, Diane Blakemore, Asa Kasher, and Dan Sperber and Deirdre Wilson.[7] For Sinclair, cognitive pragmatics develops a theory of competence that determines appropriate language use (or the competence necessary to the appropriate construction and comprehension of utterances, or indeed films).

We can only determine the aims of Odin's semio-pragmatics by contextualizing it within Metz's film theory, to which it has a complex relation. Odin re-reads and transforms Metz's work on several levels. On one level, Odin's pragmatic framework is based on the immediate discursive nature of film. This concept is influenced by Metz's famous definition that film is a *"langage sans langue,"* which places film on the side of *parole* (speech).[8] Later I shall indicate how a linguistics of *la parole* is inherently pragmatic (for it studies language use), and a linguistics of *la langue* is inherently semantic (for *la langue* constitutes language as a closed circuit, consisting of a shared system of codes).

On another level, Colin's mentalist reading of Metz's *grande syntagmatique* (to be discussed in Chapter 5) is complemented by Odin's assertion that Metz's *Language and Cinema*[9] also formalizes the spectator's competence. Odin bases this assertion on the often-quoted passage in *Language and Cinema* in which Metz compares the film semiotician's work to the film spectator's reading of a film: "The path that the semiotician follows is (ideally) parallel to that of the film *viewer*. It is the path of 'reading', not of 'composition'. But the semiotician forces himself to make explicit this procedure, step by step, while the viewer practices it directly and implicitly, wanting above all 'to understand the film'. The semiotician, for his part, would also like to be able to understand how film is understood."[10]

On the basis of this passage, Odin argues that Metz's ambition "is not to propose an immanent description of the codes of cinematic language, but to pose the framework of the cognitive work of the spectator ('to understand how film is understood'). It is interesting to note, for example, that what Metz calls 'codes,' in *Language and Cinema*, are the 'questions' that the spectator must ask when watching a film."[11]

On yet another level, Odin's semio-pragmatics combines Metz's taxonomic work in *Language and Cinema* with his psychoanalytic work. In *Psychoanalysis and Cinema: The Imaginary Signifier*,[12] Metz employed psychoanalysis to examine the general (or generic) psychic disposition the spectator adopts when watching a fiction film. He characterized this mode of attention in terms of Lacan's concept of the imaginary, which portrays the relation between fiction film and spectator as a fantasy relation. The fiction film's imaginary signifier aims to transform the spectator's consciousness – to displace her attention away from the immediate space and time of her context (including the screen's material surface) and toward the space and time of the events depicted in the diegesis (the film's fictive, imaginary elsewhere). In contrast, in *Language and Cinema*, Metz employed the taxonomic procedures of structural linguistics (among other things) to distinguish the 'system of cinematic codes' from 'filmic texts' and, within the latter category, identify the different levels at which the term 'filmic text' operates: It refers not only to individual films, but also to 'groups' and 'classes' of films.[13] Odin combines these two approaches by detailing the different modes of attention spectators adopt when watching different groups and classes of films (what Odin calls modes of film). However, Odin does not adopt a psychoanalytical approach to discuss the film spectator's psychic disposition, but a cognitive approach. The result of Odin's formulations is that the multiple modes of film, together with their multiple external constraints, create multiple dispositions, or modes of attention. Each mode of film requires a different disposition, and one of Odin's aims is to outline the different institutions that condition the various dispositions necessary to understand different modes of film.

Meaning Minus Semantics

One dramatic way to define the pragmatic theory of meaning is to say that it is premised on *non*-communication – in which *failure* to communicate is the norm, and what needs to be explained is how successful communication takes place. Less dramatically, pragmatists argue that meaning is not determined in advance, but is temporarily fixed when language is used in various contexts. By contrast, the semantic theory of meaning describes successful communication as an automatic process regulated and determined in advance by a system of codes. This system is based on the metaphor of language as a closed circuit along which messages can be encoded by the sender and decoded by the receiver, both of whom mutually share the same system of codes, ensuring no loss of meaning in the transmission of the message. Pragmatists, however, contest this model of language as a closed circuit, with sender and receiver sharing the same system of codes, because it is based on the mutual knowledge hypothesis. This hypothesis, as we saw in Chapter 2, states that knowledge is not only shared, but known to be shared, then must be known to be shared, and so on, *ad infinitum*.

Roy Harris observes that the semantic metaphor of language as a closed circuit was first developed by Ferdinand de Saussure in his *Cours de linguistique générale*: "The *Cours* is the first treatise on language to insist that speech communication is to be viewed as a 'circuit', and to attach any theoretical significance to the fact that individuals linked by this circuit act in turn as initiators of spoken messages and as recipients of such messages."[14] The metaphor of language as a 'speech circuit' borrowed two claims made by the seventeenth century psychological theories of oral communication (as developed by John Locke, and others): "(i) that communication is a process of 'telementation' (that is, of the transference of thoughts from one human mind to another), and (ii) that the necessary and sufficient condition for the successful telementation is that the process of communication, by whatever mechanisms it employs, should result in the hearer's thoughts being identical with the speaker's."[15] The concept of the speech circuit enabled Saussure to propose the existence of a system of signs shared by speaker and hearer (*la langue*), a shared system that made the speech circuit operative.

The importance for Saussure of the concept 'circuit' lay in its use of the notion of 'energy conversion' as studied within the natural sciences. It enabled language to be described scientifically in terms of a symmetry of message conversion between speaker and hearer, and Saussure needed a scientific metaphor in order to confer upon his particular object of analysis, *la langue*, scientific status. Harris remarks that the metaphor may have been suggested to Saussure during the time he presented his course in general linguistics (between 1907 and 1911) by the major technological innovations in communication, innovations that were forms of energy conversion applied to the transmission of verbal messages – telegraphy, telephony, and broadcasting. Harris is critical of Saussure's metaphor, remarking that "by presenting speech as a closed, causally determined process in every way analogous to energy-conversion processes of physics and chemistry, linguistics was provided with a forged *carte d'entrée* to the prestigious palace of modern science."[16]

One of the pragmatists' alternatives to the closed-circuit code model of communication (a model that constitutes language as a failsafe semantic algorithm) is based on the concept of inference. For pragmatists, no failsafe semantic algorithm exists between sender and receiver. The message the sender wishes to communicate cannot be automatically encoded into a message and then automatically decoded by the receiver. Instead, the sender's utterance merely modifies the cognitive environment of the receiver, and it is on the basis of this modification that the receiver infers or constructs the message the sender purportedly wishes to communicate. Pragmatists are crucially concerned with answering the question, How does the receiver infer the correct message without the benefit of a shared system of codes?

The Space of Filmic Communication

The objective of a semio-pragmatics of film and the audio-visual is to attempt to understand how audio-visual productions function in a given social space. According to this approach, the act of making or seeing a film is not immediately a fact of discourse, but a social fact obtained by adopting a *role* that regulates the production of the *film text* (which means film as a construction endowed with meaning and generating affects). A role can be described as a specific psychic positioning (cognitive and affective) that leads to the implementation of a certain number of *operations* that produce meaning and affects. *A priori*, there is absolutely no reason for the actant director and actant reader to adopt the same role (the same way of producing meaning and affects). However, it is only when the same role is adopted by these two actants that what can be called a *space of communication* is created. A space of communication is a space in which the production of meaning and affects are harmoniously formed during the filmmaking and the reading. From this space of communication derives the feeling of mutual comprehension between the actants, which gives the impression that communication resides in the transmission of a message from a Sender to a Receiver. (Roger Odin)[17]

In the middle of this long quotation, Odin states that "*a priori*, there is absolutely no reason for the actant director and actant reader to adopt the same role (the same way of producing meaning and affects)." Firstly, Odin is using A. J. Greimas's term 'actant', which designates an agent who acts or is acted upon, and Odin conceives the film spectator as an active actant, since she is designated by the term 'reader'. This sentence clearly illustrates the pragmatic dimension of Odin's work, since the activities of the actant director and actant reader are not conceived as being constrained by a closed circuit of shared codes, or, in Odin's terms, the actants are not compelled to adopt the same role. For Odin, a role is a specific psychic positioning (or mode of attention) created by the social space in which films are seen, a space consisting of 'institutions' and 'modes'. Odin employs the term 'modes' to cover what Metz calls groups and classes of films (Odin identifies eight modes in total: fiction films, documentaries, home movies, and so on). Each mode consists of several 'operations'. Throughout the 1980s, Odin identified up to seven operations (diegetization, narrativization, fictivization, and so on), which combine in different ways to constitute the different modes of film.

Collectively, these eight modes and seven operations constitute the specifically filmic dimension of the spectator's competence, the tacit knowledge necessary to the comprehension of all the various groups and classes of films. Singularly, each mode (and its specific set of operations) establishes a role that in turn constitutes the spectator's mode of attention towards that particular mode of film. In Odin's terms: "A role can be described as a specific psychic positioning (cognitive and affective) that leads to the implementation of a certain number of *operations* that produce meaning and affects." Only when the director actant and the reader actant adopt the same role (for example, when both implement the operations linked to the role established by the fictional mode) is "a *space of communication* . . . created." Adopting the same role creates the impression that semanticists believe to be pre-established – "the impression that communication resides in the transmission of a message from a Sender to a Receiver." Semanticists reify this impression of successful communication (i.e., conceive of it as a pre-given entity), whereas pragmaticists demonstrate that this impression is the result of a series of procedures. However, Odin does not give a clear and thorough account of these procedures. I shall try to explain why the actant director and actant reader adopt the same role by means of Sperber and Wilson's principle of relevance. Although Odin makes no reference to this principle, his semio-pragmatics shares most of its features (to the extent that both are cognitive theories of pragmatics) and can be effectively described within its framework.

The principle of relevance is based on the notion of maximal utility of cognitive resources. It can aid film scholars in describing the cognitive disposition a spectator needs to adopt in order to gain pleasure from watching a classical film, just as Metz in his later work employs psychoanalysis to describe the spectator's psychic disposition. The basis of Sperber and Wilson's principle of relevance lies in the relation between what they term 'contextual effect' and 'processing effort'. The addressee will process information only if it creates contextual effects – that is, if it is new and relates to information already acquired by the addressee. But the new information will not be processed at all unless the processing effort is small.

If the new information has a large contextual effect and if, at the same time, its processing effort is small, then it is what Sperber and Wilson call 'relevant'. More specifically, they define relevance in terms of two 'extent' conditions:

Extent condition 1: an assumption is relevant in a context to the extent that its contextual effects in this context are large.
Extent condition 2: an assumption is relevant in a context to the extent that the effort required to process it in this context is small.[18]

Relevance is therefore a comparative concept, involving a balancing of input (processing effort) against output (contextual effects).

Sperber and Wilson argue that, when an addressee is confronted with new information – as presented, for example, in an utterance – she processes it by generating inferences in order to complete the logical form of that utterance. Many inferences, of course, can be generated. But, in accordance with the principle of relevance, the inference the addressee generates will be the one that produces the optimal contextual effect with only a small (adequate) amount of processing effort. To communicate a particular message (or assumption), the sender produces an utterance that will be optimally relevant to the addressee. The addressee assumes the utterance is optimally relevant and will thus process it according to the principle of relevance – that is, complete it by generating an inference that enables the utterance to create the optimal contextual effect with only a small amount of processing effort.

For Sperber and Wilson, then, the principle of relevance is mutually manifest to both sender and addressee. This is because it is in the interest of the sender to communicate her message by producing an utterance that will yield in the addressee the optimal contextual effect with only a small amount of processing effort. This, of course, is also in the interest of the addressee, who will thus automatically generate the inference in which such a result can be achieved, which is precisely the inference corresponding to the sender's message.

It is therefore reasonable to assume that both sender and addressee abide by the principle of relevance when generating and processing information. Yet there is no guarantee of this, for relevance is not built into the logical structure of language, but is a contingent pragmatic principle. It is a rational but nonetheless fallible belief the sender holds about the information processing strategy of the addressee, and vice versa. In more formal terms, the inferences generated by the addressee are not deducible from the semantic content of utterances (i.e., are not demonstrative), but are non-demonstrative hypotheses always open to revision (they cannot be proved or disproved, merely confirmed or disconfirmed). Despite its contingent status, Sperber and Wilson argue, their principle of relevance is a universal cognitive-psychological principle of information processing, rather than a principle that originates in socio-cultural norms.

We can now argue that, within each of Odin's filmic modes, the textual cues make one role more relevant than other roles. We can even go on to argue that the principle of relevance constitutes the main institutional constraint on the process of making and reading a film.

Odin's binary conception of the space of communication (in which the director actant and reader actant adopt/do not adopt the same role) needs to be extended, since it is not simply a matter of either/or – either the actants' roles match up and the space of communication is created, or they don't match up, thus blocking communication. The space of communication does not simply operate on one level, as Odin suggests, but on several levels. To extend the conception of the space of communication beyond Odin's binary opposition, we can turn to David Bordwell's fourfold hierarchy of filmic meaning, as outlined in *Making Meaning*.[19] Bordwell's hierarchy consists of the following levels: (1) referential meaning (the film's diegesis, or spatio-temporal world), (2) explicit meaning (the film's conceptual meaning directly stated in the film), (3) implicit meaning (the film's symbolic or allegorical level of meaning, commonly called its theme), and (4) symptomatic meaning (the film's repressed level of meaning only involuntarily yielded by the film through its re-reading, or interpretation, by means of a master narrative, usually Marxism or psychoanalysis). Bordwell gives the example of *Psycho* to illustrate these four levels:

You might assume that *Psycho*'s referential meaning consists of its fabula and diegesis (the trip of Marion Crane from Phoenix to Fairvale, and what happens there), and you might take its explicit meaning to be the idea that madness can overcome sanity. You might then go on to argue that *Psycho*'s implicit meaning is that sanity and madness cannot be easily distinguished. ... Taken as individual expression, symptomatic meaning may be treated as the consequence of the artist's obsessions (e.g., *Psycho* as a worked over version of a fantasy of Hitchcock's). Taken as part of a social dynamic, it may be traced to economic, political, or ideological processes (for example, *Psycho* as concealing the male fear of woman's sexuality).[20]

The first three levels of meaning (referential, explicit, and implicit) are 'intentional', according to Bordwell, who develops – as I have argued in Chapters 1 and 2 – a rational-agent model of filmmaking and film reception. The space of communication can operate on any of these three levels, whether the actants operate in the same level or not. In making a film, the director actant may adopt the role constructed on the level of explicit meaning, for example, and the reader-actant may adopt the role constructed on the level of implicit meaning; but despite these different roles, a space of communication is still created. It is only when the reader-actant adopts the role constructed on the fourth level, that of symptomatic meaning (in which the 'reader-actant' identifies meaning involuntarily revealed by the text), that we see the space of communication break down (as it does in other cases – i.e., when the spectator is bored), since the reader-actant is breaking with the film's fictional contract. In

Metz's terms, such a reader-actant (who is usually a theorist) attempts to "disengage the cinema-object from the imaginary and to win it for the symbolic,"[21] that is, attempts to produce a knowledge, or a little more knowledge, of film's discursive properties, rather than reify its imaginary pleasures. Similarly, Bordwell comments, "When operating within the institution of film criticism, perceivers are likely to use the film to produce implicit and symptomatic meanings, regardless of the filmmaker's intent."[22]

Identifying different levels of meaning has not only a synchronic dimension (Bordwell's approach), but also a diachronic, or historical, dimension. In *Melodrama and Meaning*,[23] Barbara Klinger analyzes the spectators' reading strategies at different historical periods that confer upon Douglas Sirk's films different meanings: "Sirk's films have been historically characterized as subversive, adult, trash, classic, camp, and vehicles of gender identification."[24] Klinger's book is concerned with the genesis of these historical readings of Sirk's films, and, in a move that parallels Odin's work, she locates meaning in institutions (although she does not theorize the concept of the institution): "I hope to contribute to recent research focused on the manner in which institutional contexts most associated with the Hollywood cinema (such as academia, the film industry, review journalism, star publicity, and the contemporary mass media in general) create meaning and ideological identity for films."[25] In her first chapter, Klinger offers a history of how Sirk's films have been received within the academic context, concentrating on the way critics and theorists privileged Sirk's Brechtian intentions, enabling them to label moments of subversion in his American melodramas as intentional, or as forming part of the film's implicit meaning.

However, Klinger also addresses the issue of Rock Hudson's star image in Sirk's 1950s melodramas in light of his announcement in the 1980s of his homosexuality, dramatically revising his star persona as the quintessential heterosexual male. This reversal created a new level of meaning in Sirk's films: "This reversal has undoubtedly helped define contemporary responses to Sirk's films in ways totally unforeseeable by their original creators."[26] Klinger suggests here that the revision of Hudson's star persona breaks the space of communication between director actant and reader actant, since the announcement of his homosexuality creates a meaning for contemporary spectators that subverts his 1950s star persona. Running parallel to, but distinct from, the Brechtian subversion that forms part of the intentional meaning of Sirk's films, the subversion of Hudson's star persona is unintentional (does not form part of Sirk's intentional meaning). The contradiction between past star persona and present extra-filmic knowledge of Hudson's private sex life creates artifice around Hollywood's representation of heterosexual romance: "A self-reflexive and distancing element is thus introduced into the spectatorial experience of these films. As a result, Sirk's films were most likely 'made strange' in ways totally unforeseeable by him or his critics."[27]

Modes

Odin's term 'mode' encompasses Metz's divisions within the category of filmic texts – classes and groups of films. However, whereas Metz's categories remain resolutely taxonomic, Odin's modes are cognitive – they refer to a major part of each spectator's discursive competence. The space of communication is created when sender and receiver employ the same competence – the same mode – in the making and reading of a film.

In his essay "Sémio-pragmatique du cinéma et de l'audiovisuel: Modes et institutions,"[28] Odin identifies and defines – sometimes vaguely – eight different modes operative in the filmic field (several of these modes, together with examples, will be discussed later in this chapter):

1. The spectacle mode, in which the spectator perceives the film as a spectacle. Odin is using 'spectacle' in the same way that Dayan and Katz define this term in their tripartite distinction between spectacle, ceremony, and festival (see Chapter 3): Spectacle involves a minimal level of interaction between spectators and events; in this sense, film constitutes a spectacle because it minimizes interaction between the spectator and filmed events as a result of the spatio-temporal displacement inherent in films.

2. The fictional mode, in which the spectator 'resonates' to the rhythm of the narrated events (*faire vibrer au rhythme des événements racontés*). In other essays, Odin uses the phrase 'mise en phase'. Both 'resonates' and 'mise en phase' suggest that there is a *correlation* between the film-spectator relation and the relations manifest in the diegesis.

3. The 'dynamic' mode, in which the spectator 'resonates' to the rhythm of the film's sounds and images. The difference between the fictional mode and the dynamic mode is that, in the fictional mode, the spectator resonates with the diegetic events, whereas in the dynamic mode, the spectator resonates with the images and sounds as autonomous (non-representational) dimensions of the film. Odin gives the example of Moroder's version of *Metropolis*, which is colorized and has a rock soundtrack (more on this later).

4. The home movie mode, which a spectator adopts when the film depicts her – or others' – past lived experiences.

5. The documentary mode, which – in this instance at least – Odin defines as informing the spectator of real events. We shall see later that Odin also defines the documentary in terms of the real (as opposed to fictional) status of its enunciator.

6. The instructional (or persuasive) mode, from which the spectator draws a moral, or truth.

7. The artistic mode, in which the film is perceived – usually by a cinephile spectator – as the work of an auteur.

8. The aesthetic mode, in which the spectator focuses on the technical work that has gone into the creation of the images and sounds.

Collectively, these modes constitute what Odin calls "a sort of *polylectal* grammar of film,"[29] a structured heterogeneity of interacting (conflicting and overlapping) modes. This position challenges any attempt to develop *a* semiotics of *the* cinema: "The cinema as homogeneous and unique institution does not exist; there only exist cinemas relevant to different institutions: classical fiction film, instructional film."[30] Odin's concepts of modes and institutions of film attempt to challenge reductive studies that use the term 'film' in an absolute sense.

One consequence of a cognitive-pragmatic film semiotics is that the modes (and operations) are not presented as textual features embedded in films. No film is inherently a fictional, documentary, or avant-garde film, because its mode is only determined through the process of reading. A spectator who traditionally reads a film within one institution and mode can therefore read it in the context of another institution and mode. This, in fact, is what academic film scholars do when they produce symptomatic readings of films:

They study a fiction film in terms of its non-fictional context. For
Edward Branigan, this is the basis of filmic interpretation:

> It is apparent that one aim of a global interpretation is to propose (new,
> nondiegetic) contexts in which a fiction may be seen *non*fictionally, that is,
> seen to have a connection to the ordinary world. Under an interpretation,
> a fiction may offer knowledge about the real world and may come to
> possess, if not a truth value, then at least relevance, significance, appropri-
> ateness, value, plausibility, rightness, or realism.[31]

Branigan's claim is premised on the assumption that fiction establishes an indirect relation to the ordinary world, and that the practice of filmic interpretation aims to explicate that indirect relation.

Jan Simons has also expressed this pragmatic notion by arguing
that "not only do different kinds of films require from their viewers
different dispositions, but different dispositions towards the same
film are also possible."[32] Simons identifies four dispositions/modes
of attention a spectator can take toward the same film: fictivization
(in which the spectator fully engages with the film's diegetic illusion), poetic (in which the spectator focuses on the formal dimensions of a film), documentizing (in which the spectator comprehends a film in terms of her real world beliefs and extra-filmic
reality), and allegory (in which the spectator perceives a film as the
real expression of an actual director's beliefs). Simons gives the
example of Fritz Lang's *The Blue Gardenia*:

> A film like *The Blue Gardenia* for instance can be appreciated because of a
> maximal involvement in the diegetic illusion ("fictivization"), but can also
> be interpreted as Lang's comment on human fate ("allegorizing"), ana-
> lyzed and criticized as a document of sexist and patriarchal ideology ("doc-
> umentization"), but also an example of exercises in style ("poetic").[33]

It is instructive to compare this fourfold reading of *The Blue Gardenia* with Bordwell's fourfold characterization of *Psycho*: The most
direct overlap is between Bordwell's implicit meaning and Simons's
allegorizing reading, and Bordwell's symptomatic meaning and Simons's documentization. Both frameworks outline 'how to do
things with filmic texts', although Simons is clear to state (as does
Odin) that no spectator is free to read any film within any institution and mode, because of contextual constraints. In other words,
something like the principle of relevance guides this pragmatic
process. (However, Bordwell maintains that a symptomatic reading

simply involves the arbitrary imposition of theoretical frameworks onto films.)

After outlining the main modes of filmmaking, Odin goes on to characterize the specificity of each mode in terms of a combination of operations.

Operations

In his latest essays, Odin identifies six operations, which he groups under three categories. In earlier work, he identified up to seven operations and simply listed them, one by one. Here I shall first present Odin's list of seven operations and then his more recent reformulations, briefly noting any major differences between early and later work.

Odin identifies the characteristics of each operation and emphasizes that no mode (and, therefore, no single filmic text belonging to that mode) simply embodies one operation (operations cannot, therefore, be identified with single films). In his essay "Du spectateur fictionalisant au nouveau spectateur: approche sémio-pragmatique"[34] Odin lists the following operations:

1. Figurativization
2. Diegetization
3. Narrativization
4. Monstration
5. Belief
6. Mise en phase
7. Fictivization

Figurativization. It is the most general – or least specific – operation and is responsible for visual analogy. Figurativization also constitutes a procedure in Greimassian semiotics, in which it is defined more precisely than in Odin's work: "It is necessary to distinguish . . . at least two levels of figurativization procedures: the first is that of *figuration*, that is, of the setting-up of semiotic figures (a sort of phonological level); the second would be that of *iconization*, which aims at decking out the figures exhaustively so as to produce the referential illusion which would transform them into images of the world."[35] Umberto Eco's analysis of iconic signs into ten discrete codes organized in terms of a triple articulation went

some way to detailing both figuration (the ten codes) and iconization (their triple articulation).[36]

Diegetization. This operation involves the construction of an imaginary world inhabited by characters. It refers to the literal dimension of the film – the space, time, and events experienced by
characters. (As such, it presupposes the prior operation of figurativization.) In Bordwell's terminology, diegetization operates on a
film's most basic level – referential meaning. Odin emphasizes that
diegetization is an operation constituting part of the director actant's and reader actant's discursive competence, suggesting that
the literal level of filmic meaning is not simply embedded in the
film, but is part of an actant's judgment. Edward Branigan comes
to a similar conclusion: "Diegesis is not something that the film
either possesses or lacks, but rather is a way of describing an inter-
locking set of judgments we make about the presentation of sensory
data in the film at a particular moment."[37]

Narrativization. To make the concept of narrativization specific,
Odin distinguishes between the 'narrative effect' and the story.[38]
Whereas the 'narrative effect' is a micro-narrative element and can
be found in the most abstract, avant-garde films, the story refers to
a film's overall (or macro) narrative structure. Furthermore, Odin
characterizes the story in Greimassian terms as two complete actantial structures:

It seems, in particular, that all stories require at least the intervention of
two antagonistic Subjects (a Subject and an Anti-Subject), and therefore,
since there is no Subject without an Addresser and without an Object, no
operational Subject without a Helper, and no Object without an Addressee,
two complete actantial structures (one for the Subject, the other for the
Anti-Subject).[39]

We have seen that diegetization presupposes figurativization. However, diegetization does not presuppose narrativization, since the
construction of an imaginary world can be organized around description rather than narration. But narrativization cannot operate
without diegetization, since the two actantial structures that constitute narrativization require an imaginary world in which to function.

Odin refers to Gerard Genette's claim that narration does not exist in the cinema because of absence of a mediator who introduces a distance between the activity of telling and the story told.[40] Genette's claim is based on the analogical nature of the filmic image (on its operation of figurativization). However, Odin refers to two further operations (belief and monstration) that challenge Genette's claim.

Belief. Any reference to this concept today must go beyond the facile gloss that film viewing is based upon a 'suspension of disbelief', for, as John Searle has argued: "Every subject matter has its catchphrases to enable us to stop thinking before we have got a solution to our problems. . . . It is easy to stop thinking about the logical status of fictional discourse if we repeat slogans like 'the suspension of disbelief' or expressions like 'mimesis'. Such notions contain our problem but not its solution."[41] The notion of suspension of disbelief is based upon the splitting of the spectator actant's psychic disposition, in which her attention is drawn away from (or in which she disavows) the mediator. The notion is therefore useful in refuting Genette's claim, but does not sufficiently characterize the spectator's mode of attention.

Richard Allen has clarified film theory's facile gloss of the concept of disavowal as the 'suspension of disbelief' by distinguishing between normal and pathological forms of disavowal, and by disengaging the concept of disavowal from the concept of fetishism.[42] These two aims are, of course, interrelated, because pathological disavowal is based upon fetishism and involves a fundamental contradiction in the spectator's beliefs – what Freud called a splitting of the ego – in which one set of beliefs are conscious and an antithetical set are unconscious. (This is the form of disavowal traditionally adopted by psychoanalytic film theorists.) Normal disavowal, on the other hand, is benign and does not involve a contradiction of beliefs. In the cinema, this means that pathological disavowal involves a spectator's actually believing in the reality of a fiction film's illusion, whereas normal disavowal involves the spectator's merely entertaining in thought the fiction film's illusion while all the time knowing that it is an illusion. In normal disavowal the spectator remains a conscious, rational agent, whereas pathological disavowal involves a conflict between a spectator's conscious and unconscious reactions to a fiction film:

A spectator of a given disposition might respond to a film as if it were real and behave as if the world on the screen and the world of experience formed an undifferentiated continuum. Fraught with the anxiety correlative to such an acting out of fantasy, his pathological spectator would at once ward off the anxiety and keep his experience intact through a splitting of the ego: I know this is a film, but all the same I believe it to be real. A case like this may illuminate the character of cinemagoing in general, but it would be absurd to claim that this is really the way in which the cinema spectator characteristically behaves. . . . The movies do not cause the ego to lose its grip on reality and unconsciously defend against this loss by splitting.[43]

Monstration. Odin borrows this term from André Gaudreault, for whom it means 'to show', and who opposes it to 'narration' (to narrate).[44] Furthermore, monstration is equated with spatial representation and the theater, and narration with temporal representation and written (or scriptural) narrative. For Gaudreault, cinema combines monstration and narration, since the shot shows space, whereas the cut (and, more generally, editing) introduces temporal and narrative articulation between shots.

Mise en Phase. This concept has undergone significant transformation in Odin's work. He first introduced it in his 1983 paper "Mise en phase, déphasage et performitivé dans *Le Tempestaire* de Jean Epstein."[45] All of the three concepts found in the title of the essay function to specify different relations established between the film and the spectator. Mise en phase designates the moments in a film when the relation between film and spectator 'resonates' with the relations manifest in the film's diegesis: "The homogeneity between the positioning of the spectator and of the narrative dynamic manifest in the diegesis constitutes one of the essential characteristics of the functioning of the fiction film (one of the *operations* of the *fiction-effect*)."[46] Mise en phase is not to be equated with the conjunction between film and spectator. Instead, it involves a correlation between the film-spectator relation and the relations manifest in the diegesis. In other words, mise en phase is created when a conjunction within the diegesis is matched by a conjunction in the film-spectator relation, and also when a disjunction in the diegesis is matched by a disjunction in the film-spectator relation. In this way, the spectator is said to resonate to the rhythm of the events told.

Odin offers two examples of mise en phase in "Du spectateur fictionalisant":

> If the operation of mise en phase has a meaning, it is just a matter of mobilizing all the materials of film – rhythm, music, all the dynamics of montage, all the plays on looks and framings, etc. – to make the spectator 'resonate' to the rhythm of the narrated events. Thus, a shipwreck scene [in order to create mise en phase] will be filmed using blurred images, staccato camera movements, misframings, etc. to the point of illegibility, to realize in the film-spectator relation the aggressivity manifest in the storm. ... Inversely, carefully framed long shots, a softly filtered light delicately modelling faces, a 'poetic' type of dialogue (with rhythm, assonances, timing), a diction directly anchoring speech in the musical inflections, will make the spectator feel an extraordinary complicity with the secrecy between characters, as in the admirable scene in *Partie de campagne* where Henriette and Juliette confide in one another under the cherry tree.[47]

By creating resonance, mise en phase functions as the principle of intelligibility in the cinema, for it designates a correlation between textual structures and spectator competence – with one miming or echoing the other.

Déphasage, or phase displacement, simply designates the opposite, in which the relation manifest in the diegesis (conjunction or disjunction) is not mirrored in the film-spectator relation. The spectator does not, therefore, resonate with the diegetic events. According to Odin, phase displacement is created in *Le Tempestaire* through Epstein's use of non-professional actors, who never conform to the impression of reality evident in other fiction films. For Odin, this alienates many spectators, leading to the breaking of the fiction effect (since, as Odin points out in the preceding excerpt, mise en phase is one of the important operations of the fiction effect). The choice spectators face is then simply to condemn the film as badly made or to comprehend the use of non-professional actors as a reflexive device, drawing attention to filmic discourse, rather than to story. Odin takes the second option, arguing that *Le Tempestaire* is reflexive – or, in his terms, it is a performative text. Later we shall see that, in his later work, Odin distinguishes between two types of mise en phase (fictional and dynamic) and changes its status.

Fictivization. Unlike the other operations Odin discusses, fictivization is unique to one mode of film – the fiction film. The function

of this operation is to confer a fictional status upon the enunciator
and addressee of a fiction film:

Fictivization is a modality which is applied to the enunciative structure of
film, an intentional modality that characterizes the status, or position, the
spectator attributes to the fiction film's enunciator. Fictivization consists of
considering that the enunciator does not intervene as a 'real origin' but as
a fictive origin: it accomplishes the act of enunciation 'without assuming
the commitments which are normally required for this act' [John Searle].[48]

Similarly, "the spectator no longer feels interpellated as a real person having to take seriously what is narrated to him."[49]

Odin characterizes fictivization in Greimassian terms as a modality – that is, in terms of the subject's modification of meaning
according to its mode of existence. In fictivization, the modification
of the film's meaning derives from the enunciator's modalization
as fictive, and the reader actant's modalization as imaginary. The
result is that the addressee need not take as serious (as real) the
meanings articulated in the film, but comprehend these meanings
in terms of non-deceptive pretense. Documentary film's meaning is
modalized differently: Both enunciator and reader actant are modalized as real, with the result that the addressee must take seriously
what is articulated on screen. One consequence of this theory is
that the fictive/documentary character of a film is determined, not
by the (un)reality of the profilmic events, but by the modal status
attributed to the addressee and enunciator. Within a semio-
pragmatic framework, a film's status is defined in terms of its mode
of address and the modality conferred upon its enunciator.

Odin defines the fictional mode of film as possessing all seven
operations, which combine to create what he calls the 'fiction effect'
(and what Noël Burch significantly calls the Institutional Mode of
Representation). Other modes are defined by the presence or absence of these various operations.

In his 1994 essay "Sémio-pragmatique du cinéma et de l'audiovisuel: Modes et institutions,"[50] Odin identifies the following
three types of operations:

(a) Operations concerning the representational status of images and
    sounds
(b) Discursive operations (diegetization, narrativization, discursivi-
    zation)

(c) Enunciative operations (construction of an enunciative structure), which includes the status conferred upon the dominant enunciator

Category (a) simply refers to 'figurativization' (operation 1 in the earlier list); category (b) refers to operations 2, 3, and 4 (it seems that Odin has exchanged Gaudreault's term 'monstration' for the more general term 'discursivization'); category (c) refers directly to operation 7, 'fictivization', and all reference to 'belief structures' is dropped. The main difference in Odin's reformulation is that mise en phase is divided into two categories: the fictional and the dynamic. Furthermore, fictional mise en phase is defined as the result of all the other operations (it is equated with the fiction effect, rather than being conceived as one operation among others that lead to the fiction effect).

Institutions

A priori, the spectator can make any mode function on any film (or fragment of film); in reality, we are always subject to constraints that limit this possibility. *Textual* constraints: all films tend to block the working of certain modes of production of meaning and affects; *contextual* constraints: seeing a film is always made in an institutional framework which governs our way of producing meaning and affects. In fact, . . . these two types of constraint can be reduced to one: *institutional* constraints.[51]

The space of filmic communication is delimited, in the final analysis, by institutions. The starting point of Odin's reflections on institutions is (not surprisingly) the work of Metz. For Metz, institutions consist of two dimensions, one mentalistic and internal, the other material and external: "The institution is outside us and inside us, indistinctively collective and intimate, sociological and psychoanalytic, just as the general prohibition of incest has as its individual corollary the Oedipus complex, castration or perhaps in other states of society different psychical configurations, but one which still *imprint* the institution in us in their own way."[52] For Odin, the external and material dimension of institutions consists of the places in which the film is projected – commercial cinemas (for films realized within the fictional, spectacle, and dynamic modes), art house cinemas (films of the aesthetic and artistic modes), schools (films of the instructional mode) and so on – whereas the internal and mentalistic dimension comprises the modes and operations constituting each spectator's discursive competence, which determine the appropriate mode of attention necessary to the comprehension of a film.[53] Odin adds that each film is to some extent imprinted with an institutional identity, and he specifies two procedures of inscription: the film's display of its 'preferred' institution in its credit sequence and the spectator's recognition in the film of a thematic and stylistic system characteristic of a certain mode of a certain institution. Furthermore, as mentioned in the discussion of modes, the reading of a film is also determined by the principle of relevance. This principle encourages a cinephile to allegorize an auteurist film, whereas its fictionalization is the preferred reading of 'naive' (non-cinephile) spectators; film academics work against the principle of relevance in order to study a film's form or to produce a symptomatic reading (leading to a deliberate break in the space of filmic communication).

Each institution consists of several modes – for example, the institution of commercial cinema comprises the spectacle, fictional, and dynamic modes, whereas the institution of non-professional cinema includes the home movie, aesthetic, and artistic modes. Institutions determine the mode in which a particular film is to be comprehended. For Odin, an institution is "a bundle of determinations which govern the production of meaning in selecting, hierarchising, and structuring the modes of production of meaning which are put to work."[54]

Finally, just as no operation is specific to a particular mode (with the exception of fictivization), no mode is specific to a particular institution. The relations among institutions, modes, and operations are relations of inclusion: Operations are included in modes, and modes are included in institutions. Figure 5 presents a summary of the main institutions, modes, and operations that Odin identifies.

The Documentary, Home Movie, and 'Dynamic' Modes of Filmmaking

The Documentary Mode. As pointed out, for Odin, the only essential difference between the fiction and documentary modes of film lies in the operation of fictivization – the modal status conferred upon the enunciator and addressee. In the fiction film, the enunciator and addressee are modalized as imaginary (or absent), whereas

---

INSTITUTIONS

External:
commercial cinemas, schools,
art house cinemas, etc.

Internal:
discursive competence
(comprising modes and operations)

MODES
spectacle, fictional, dynamic, home movies,
documentary, instructional, artistic

OPERATIONS
figurativization, diegetization, narrativization,
monstration, belief, mise en phase, fictivization

Fig. 5

---

in the documentary, they are modalized as real. Here I shall develop this idea further, with particular reference to Odin's essay "Film documentaire, lecture documentarisante."[55]

Firstly, in distinguishing fiction from documentary modes of filmmaking, Odin notes that the documentary film has no privileged relation to reality, since both modes employ the same technologies – mechanics, optics, and photochemistry. All modes that employ these technologies therefore record real events. The fiction mode, for example, is a record of actions and events performed by actors at a certain time in a certain place (either on location or in a studio). Rejecting a "semiotics of realization" as a criterion for defining the documentary mode, Odin instead opts for a "semiotics of reading" to define its specificity.[56] In Greimassian terms, Odin rejects a referential theory of truth (study of the relation between signs and their extra-textual reality) for a study of veridiction – the modality of truth/reality as articulated by enunciator and addressee.[57] Most of Odin's essay is concerned with characterizing the specificity of the documentary mode according to the documentarizing reading strategy adopted by film spectators, and with outlining how this documentarizing reading is triggered by the film and the institutions in which it is screened.

To posit an imaginary/absent enunciator for the fictional mode involves not only the text's concealing its own marks of enunciation (the film as *histoire*) but, more radically, the spectator's refusing to posit the existence of any process of enunciation at all. The first is an internal constraint, the second an external constraint: "The opposition 'story' vs 'discourse' is an effect of the text (it is identifiable through the marks inscribed in the utterance), whereas the opposition fictivizing reading vs documentarizing reading is an effect of the positioning of the reader facing the film, the result of an operation external to the film: a strictly pragmatic operation."[58] As noted, because of its pragmatic status, the mode of reading adopted by the reader actant is not tied to one mode of filmmaking. The documentarizing reading is therefore one level on which spectators can read any mode of filmmaking; it is not a reading strategy limited to one mode. But the documentarizing reading is privileged only in films generated by the documentary mode and institution. Odin begins to consider textual cues that privilege the documentarizing reading in the documentary film.

Firstly, he considers the different types of real enunciators that spectators can posit:[59]

1. The reader can take the camera to be the real enunciator. In this framework, all the profilmic events are subjected to the documentarizing reading. Odin finds the best example of this argument in the work of Siegfried Kracauer.
2. The reader can take the cinema (or the cinematic apparatus) to be the real enunciator. Here, Odin refers to the work of Stephen Heath.
3. The reader can take as the real enunciator the society in which the film is produced. Although it is not noted by Odin, this position can be attributed to theorists who practice symptomatic interpretations, particularly those who take symptomatic meaning to be part of economic, political, or ideological processes of the social dynamic. In the *Psycho* example discussed earlier, the enunciator of the film is deemed to be patriarchy, which attempts to conceal male fear of woman's sexuality.
4. The reader can take the cameraperson to be the film's real enunciator. (This category, which is usually applied to the reportage film, will be discussed later.)
5. The reader can take the director to be the enunciator, as auteur critics do. In Bordwell's terms, an auteurist reading operates on the implicit level of meaning, since auteur critics are not compre-

hending the text literally, but allegorically. This is a non-fictional reading to the extent that auteur critics are reading the film as part of an actual director's oeuvre.

6. Finally, the reader can take the specialist responsible for the film to be its enunciator, a reading strategy relevant to instructional films, for example.

Despite the pragmatic account Odin offers of the reader's construction of these various enunciators, his most persuasive example, relating to the reportage film, is primarily a textual account. In reportage films, a number of specific textual figures prompt the reader to take the cameraperson as the embodiment of the real enunciator. These figures include a blurred image, jolting camera movements, hesitant pan shots, abrupt editing, long sequence shots, insufficient light, film grain, direct sound (as opposed to studio sound), and real background ambience. (Odin notes that these figures are also imitated by fiction films that want to look like reportage films.) These textual figures serve as an index of the cameraperson's real presence:

The function of this set of figures is clear: to mark in the very structure of the film the real existence of the cameraman; to make known to the reader that the cameraman is to be taken as the real Enunciator. The figures cited testify to the difficulty the cameraman had filming in the conditions he found himself in, and to his physical interaction with the event, to see the risks he took.[60]

Whereas the technical perfection of many fiction films enables the reader to posit the enunciator as imaginary or absent, the documentary film (and reportage film in particular) signifies its concrete and contingent location in the profilmic world. In other words, the cameraperson is always locatable or grounded on a specific point, and it is this anchoring in a specific point that leads the spectator to infer a real enunciator (a hand-held camera, for example, marks the actual anchoring of the cameraperson in the space and time of the events she is filming). In news bulletins, the cameraperson is subject to the forces of the events she is filming; she does not exist outside or apart from the events being filmed, but is subject to their laws. She can therefore attest to the existence of the events filmed, and the preceding textual figures act as an index of her presence, her status as witness. This in turn modalizes the addressee as a real spectator – as one who must take seriously what is presented to her.

The Home Movie Mode. The study of the home movie seems to be one of Odin's greatest passions, and also the motivation for his work: "It is, at least in part, because of this work on the home movie that I came to experience the necessity of constructing a semio-pragmatic model [of film]."[61] Here I shall present an overview of Odin's work on the operations that characterize the home movie, making particular reference to his essay "Rhétorique du film de famille."[62]

The institutional characteristic of the home movie is that it is shown within the domestic space, in which both the enunciator and addressees are family members: "A home movie is a film made by a member of a family, with regard to objects or events linked in one way or another to the history of this family, and for the privileged viewing by members of this family."[63] Odin then discusses eight textual characteristics that prompt the spectator to read a film as a home movie:[64]

1. The absence of closure (the film does not embody the operation of narrativization).
2. Discontinuous linear temporality. The home movie is dedicated to chronological order (there are no flashbacks, flashforwards, or alternating montage); however, that chronology is indeterminate (the temporal relations between the fragments of the home movie are discontinuous). The home movie does not, therefore, embody the operation of diegetization.
3. Spatial indeterminacy. As with (2), the operation of diegetization is not adhered to because it is often difficult to determine the spatial relation between shots.
4. Dispersed narrative. This point is a continuation of (1); not only does the home movie lack closure, but its narrative elements do not constitute a macro-narrative (it therefore only contains micronarrative elements).
5. Jumps. The home movie disregards the 180 degree axis of action line and ignores the 30 degree rule, shot/reverse shot, and the other codes of spatial coherence. As with (2) and (3), this textual figure signifies a disregard for the operation of diegetization.
6. Blurred images, jolting camera movements, hesitant pan shots,

and so on. As with the reportage film, the enunciator of the home movie is modalized as real. However, Odin resists comparing the home movie to the reportage film, because they are shown in different institutions.

7. Address to the camera. The family members in home movies frequently look at the camera, thus blocking the fiction effect by acknowledging its presence (the camera and its operator are therefore located in the diegesis through acknowledgement by a direct address).

8. The sound of a home movie may be inaudibe, variable, or completely absent, with the effect – as with (2), (3), and (5) – that it only presents fragments of a diegesis (nonconformity to the operation of diegetization).

Odin then returns to a pragmatic perspective on the home movie to discuss in more detail its relation to the operation of diegetization. From a pragmatic perspective, the diegesis not only is conceived as a textual construction, but is also a product of the spectator's competence. If the home movie is projected in its institutional context (in the domestic space of the family who is represented), then we can argue that the operation of diegetization is put fully into effect. Odin notes, "The home movie, in fact, has as its particularity to be made to be *seen* by those who have lived (or seen) what is represented on the screen."[65] The home movie itself does not need to establish a coherent diegesis because the events filmed are already known by the intended addressees. All the home movie needs to do is revive the addressee's memory of the actual experiences. The home movie recalls a previous series of events; it does not need to narrate those events. The absence of the operations of diegetization and narrativization is therefore an essential characteristic of the home movie, and this is why Odin is critical of ciné-clubs that encourage home movie makers to adopt the techniques of the fictional mode. It is only outsiders (non–family members) who experience the home movies of others as fragmented. Operating within its intended institution, the home movie can function without the need for the operations of diegetization and narrativization. This leads Odin to state the paradox generated by the home movie: For the relevant members of the family, the home movie generates pleasure through the diegetic and narrative poverty of its images. By not presenting the addressee with a complete and coherent diegesis, the home movie has less chance of conflict with, or contradict, the addressee's experience.

Finally, Odin rather confusingly ends his analysis of the home movie by arguing that it is still involved in the creation of a fiction, despite the fact that it does not embody all the operations necessary for the creation of the fiction effect. The home movie creates a fictional representation of a particular family through its selective portrayal of events in that family's life – the special occasions and anniversaries, rather than everyday reality. The home movie functions to guarantee the institution of the family (and this is why, in French, the home movie is called *film de famille*): "The home movie is not an innocent film; it contributes in its own way to the maintenance of a certain order."[66] However, I do not think we should understand Odin's use of the term 'fiction' in the context of the home movie to mean the same as the fiction effect as defined earlier. The home movie's creation of a fiction involves its presentation of an imaginary unity (the family) rather than its utilization of the mode of attention a spectator adopts when watching a fiction film (the mode of attention that encourages the spectator to read the film in front of her as a fiction film).

The Dynamic Mode. In the second half of his essay "Du spectateur fictionalisant," after outlining the seven operations that constitute the fiction effect, Odin writes about the emergence of the 'dynamic' mode of filmmaking, which derives from the institution of commercial cinema. Although shown in commercial cinemas, films belonging to the dynamic mode do not create the fiction effect, because they do not embody all of its operations. Odin mentions films such as *Star Wars, Tron, Cobra*, and the *Mad Max* and *Rocky* series but gives particular attention to Moroder's modified version of Lang's *Metropolis*.

Odin charts the modifications that transformed this film from one conforming to the fictional mode to one conforming to the dynamic mode. The main difference between these two modes is that, in the fictional mode, the spectator resonates with the narrated events and, in the dynamic mode, resonates with the sounds and images. In the terminology established in Chapter 2, the dynamic mode operative in Moroder's *Metropolis* prevents the spectator from comprehending Lang's *Metropolis* in terms of the container schema, since the spectator cannot enter into the diegetic space of the new version of *Metropolis*.

Moroder's modifications, which transformed *Metropolis* from a fiction to a dynamic film, include the addition of tinting, the re-writing of intertitles, the addition (sometimes in the form of still photographs) of new material edited out of the original version and the introduction of a rock music soundtrack. For Odin, all these modifications work to block the fiction effect: In fact, he argues that six of the seven operations listed in the first half of his essay are affected, and only figurativization remains intact.

Odin argues that whereas black and white contributes to diege-tization and the effect of depth, colorizing a film today draws attention to film as film: "Colorization appears to be a process of derealization opposing at the same time monstration, diegetization, and belief. With colorization, the 'image effect' takes over from the 'fiction effect'."[67] The spectator's look does not go beyond the sur-face of the image into the imaginary elsewhere of the film's die-gesis, but remains on the surface of the image. We can say that the transformation taking place from the fictional mode to the dynamic mode is that between a gaze aesthetic and a glance aesthetic, re-spectively.

With the addition of still photographs into the film, a rupture of the impression of movement takes place. Many of these still photo-graphs are filmed by using a moving camera, a technique that, for Odin, simply highlights the absence of movement in the images. Furthermore, the manipulation of the intertitles (making the letters dynamic, and so on) draws attention to them as lettering. In gen-eral, the plastic elements in the image track have a semi-autonomous status in relation to the operation of narrativization; they do not function to further the film's narrative.

But it is primarily the addition of a rock music soundtrack that transforms *Metropolis* into a film belonging to the dynamic mode. Odin argues that the organization of the soundtrack into musical movements opposes the original film's organization into narrative segments, with the result that the story merely illustrates the soundtrack, rather than the reverse, as is the case in films of the fictional mode. One technique that privileges sound over image is what Odin calls 'fine' (or micro-) synchronization. In films of the fictional mode, synchronization between extra-diegetic music and the story only operates on the macro level, whereas diegetic sound and music are synchronized on the micro level.[68] But in Moroder's *Metropolis*, the non-diegetic music is synchronized with the story, with the result that small actions in the story – particularly gestures – are synchronized to the rock soundtrack. A non-fictional dimension of the film (the rock music soundtrack) seems to be conjoined to a fictional dimension (character action). For Odin, this blocks the operations of narrativization and diegetization and aligns Moroder's *Metropolis* with other films dominated by the soundtrack: "It is this relation (micro-synchronization of the elements of the image which are not sources of the sound) that dominates in dance films, musical comedies, opera films, burlesque films."[69]

Odin conceives a reversal taking place in Moroder's *Metropolis*, in which its narrative is a mere adjunct to the plastic elements of the image and soundtrack. The result is that "the film acts directly on the spectator, a spectator who no longer resonates with the narrated events (the fiction-effect) but resonates with the variations of rhythm, intensity and color of the images and sounds."[70] In the dynamic mode, the space of filmic communication is not governed by the production of meaning but by the production of affects.

Odin ends his analysis of Moroder's *Metropolis* by generalizing about the dynamic mode of filmmaking and the new spectator it constructs. He links the emergence of the dynamic mode to the decline in the role of fiction, metanarratives, and the end of the social in postmodern culture. However, it is equally possible to take his argument in another direction: to link it to the more traditional genre of the decorative arts. Bordwell has established a mode of filmmaking called parametric (or style-centred) narration by referring to Gombrich's work on decorative arts: "Borrowing from E. H. Gombrich's account of decorative art, I have argued that 'parametric' films organize film techniques in patterns that may create an ongoing spectatorial engagement independent of narrative action. The films of Yasujiro Ozu, with their nonnarrative structures of locale and shot composition, offer good examples of what Gombrich calls order without meaning."[71] Bordwell also refers to the serial music of Messiaen, Pierre Boulez, Karlheinz Stockhausen, Luigi Nono, and Jean Barraqué, together with the work of the *nouveaux romanciers*, as other instances of style-centred artistic practices.[72] Bordwell also notes that parametric narration in the cinema "is not linked to a single national school, period, or genre of filmmaking. . . . In many ways, the pertinent historical context is less that of filmmaking than that of film theory and criticism. To some extent, then, this mode of narration applies to isolated filmmakers and fugitive films."[73] For this reason, it is possible to consider the dynamic mode of filmmaking to be a style-centred form of cinema operating within the context of New Hollywood Cinema, rather than to be a symptom of the end of fiction and the social.

Theories of pragmatics focus critical attention away from texts in themselves and toward the actants that create and 'use' these texts. By means of the concepts of 'institution', 'mode', and 'operation', Odin is able to avoid falling into the trap of positing the actants as the sole producers of filmic meaning. Instead, for Odin, the actants are simply points of passage for a multitude of determinations. Nonetheless, Odin's conception of actants requires refinement, especially in the light of comments made earlier concerning Bordwell's discussion of symptomatic meaning in *Psycho* and Simons's gloss on a documentizing reading of *The Blue Gardenia*. In brief, it is misleading to modalize actants (the enunciator and addressee) of the fictional mode of filmmaking as imaginary/absent and the actants of the documentary mode as real. A symptomatic/documentizing reading of a fiction film will posit its actants as real – although on a latent level – since this type of reading attempts to relate that fiction film to its real, socio-historical context (usually capitalism and patriarchy).

This suggests that whereas documentaries modalize their actants as real on the surface level, fiction films modalize their actants as real on a latent level. This reformulation enables us to begin refining our understanding of the relation between fiction and reality. As I mentioned in the introduction to this chapter, for Odin fiction and documentary films are separated by only one operation, that of fictivization. If my suggestion, that the fiction film's actants are modalized as real on the latent level, whereas in documentaries they are modalized as real on the surface level, is viable, this would suggest that fiction and documentaries are even closer to one another, since the operation of fictivization would not separate them.[74] Both fiction and documentaries are attempting to achieve the same aim, although on different levels: Both are attempting to represent social reality, but fiction achieves this end in an indirect manner. Fiction is not to be opposed to reality, but is a means by which reality can be indirectly represented.

Here we reach an anthropological discussion of fiction, an under-developed area in film studies at the present time. In literary theory, however, Wolfgang Iser has recently developed a study of literary anthropology.[75] Iser does not ask, What is fiction?, but Why do we need fiction?[76] For Iser, only a pragmatic (rather than a semantic) response will adequately answer this question. Whereas semantics is confined to offering a definition of fiction's explanatory function free of its context (situation), a pragmatic answer addresses the contextual impact of fiction: "Impacting as the pragmatics of fiction never loses sight of its situational function, whereas explanation as the semantics of fiction aims precisely to make its situational necessity disappear. Thus the pragmatic function unfolds the special use of fiction, and the special use determines the individual nature of fiction."[77] One pragmatic function of fiction, noted previously, is defined by its relation to reality: It can present a simplified image of a complex reality, but can also go beyond the given into the realm of the potential or unrealized. Odin's proclamation of the end of the social and the fictional is unfounded because, if we take a pragmatic definition of fiction to its logical conclusion (that is, take it into the realm of anthropology), we see that it is an anthropological constant. Rather than positing its disappearance, it is more accurate to argue that the function of fiction (together with the function of the social) is constantly renewed by successive generations.

CHAPTER FIVE

All in the Mind?

The Cognitive Status of Film Grammar

> The problem for the linguist... is to determine from the data of performance the underlying system of rules that has been mastered by the speaker-hearer and that he puts to use in actual performance. Hence, in the technical sense, linguistic theory is mentalistic, since it is concerned with discovering a mental reality underlying actual behavior. (Noam Chomsky)[1]

> My aim... is to argue for what I will gladly call a *grammar of film*, and adhere at the same time to a conception of scientific work broadly comparable to that of Metz (and [Sol] Worth), but advancing different theses as to the general nature of rules committed to representing this model of the structure of film. (Dominique Chateau)[2]

One indication that linguistics has become a mature science is its ability to handle in a formalized manner the problem of 'grammaticality', or to define in formal terms the boundary between 'grammatical' and 'ungrammatical' sentences. A technical formulation of this boundary was one of Noam Chomsky's primary aims in his transformational generative grammar (TGG). We can claim that film theory has reached a relatively mature stage (in comparison with other disciplines in the humanities) thanks in part to attempts to develop a film 'grammar' based on Chomsky's early theories of TGG.

David Bordwell has expressed his surprise "that theorists who assign language a key role in determining subjectivity have almost completely ignored the two most important contemporary developments in linguistic theory: Chomsky's Transformational Generative Grammar and his Principles-and-Parameters theory."[3] In this chapter I shall focus on two cognitive film semioticians – Michel Colin and Dominique Chateau – who have, contrary to Bordwell's assertion, been working with Chomsky's theories since the early seventies. One conclusion we can draw from their work is that Metz's *grande syntagmatique* (GS) does not merely observe and organize filmic data, but formalizes in a set of explicit rules the film spectator's competence, or intuitive knowledge of film.

We saw in Chapter 2 how Michel Colin returned to Metz's semiotic theory of film and subjected it to a cognitive re-reading, transforming it into a cognitive semantics of film. In this chapter we shall review how Colin re-read Metz's *grande syntagmatique* from a cognitive perspective. Colin's re-reading is heavily influenced by what is generally known as the Standard Theory of transformational generative grammar (TGG), as presented by Chomsky in *Aspects of the Theory of Syntax*. After outlining the basic components of Chomsky's Standard Theory and presenting Colin's long and detailed Chomskyan re-reading of Metz's GS, I shall focus on the way 'deviant' film sequences (those that seem to break the implicit grammatical rules of film) are comprehended. I shall end by considering the cognitive status of Metz's GS.

Transformational Generative Grammar

The fundamental principle of TGG is elegant in its simplicity. TGG answers the question, How can a language user understand a potentially infinite number of sentences? Infinity has no boundaries or limits and cannot therefore be understood in human terms. In other words, it has no cognitive reality. TGG reduces this infinity to a finite series of steps, which can be understood in human terms. In other words, these finite steps have a cognitive reality. A TGG of film also begins with the issue of how a film spectator can understand a potentially infinite number of films and similarly reduces this infinity to a finite series of steps.

In TGG, what are these finite steps? The elegance of the Standard Theory lies in the following components: It includes a finite set of recursive rules that generate deep structure 'sentences' (or basic strings) and a finite number of transformational rules that transform these deep structures into a potentially infinite number of surface structure sentences. Moreover, the grammar must be constrained so that it generates *all* and *only* the sentences that native speakers judge to be well formed, or grammatical. So, for Chomsky, 'grammatical' is a technical, rather than an evaluative or prescriptive term. In this technical sense, a grammatical sentence is one that is generated according to the rules of a particular grammar (it is a sentence recognized by that grammar). Such a sentence can thereby be described as well formed with reference to that grammar.

The grammar generates deep structures by means of a series of re-writing (or categorical) rules, which expand a single grammatical category into a string of other grammatical categories, such as

$$S \rightarrow NP + VP$$
$$NP \rightarrow Det + N$$

This reads, Re-write Sentence as Noun Phrase and Verb Phrase, and re-write Noun Phrase as Determiner and Noun. Re-writing rules can be represented in the form of a tree diagram. Tree diagrams interrelate three elements: a root node (the topmost node); preterminal nodes, which are dominated by the root node; and terminal nodes (the lexical entries). At the end of re-writing rules, the category symbols are replaced by lexical entries (e.g., the category symbol N is re-written as a particular noun). Strings containing grammatical categories are called preterminal strings, whereas those containing lexical entries are called terminal strings (see Figure 6).

Category symbols such as N cannot simply be re-written as any lexical entry belonging to the class of nouns. Each category symbol is analyzable into a set of complex symbols, a set of specified selectional features. Thus, a particular noun category symbol may be represented in terms of the following selectional features: [+N, +Common, +Count, +Animate, −Human]. Only a noun that possesses these particular selectional features (such as 'dog' 'cat') can then be inserted into the preterminal string to form a terminal string. The selectional features therefore act as restrictions, for they specify the constraints placed on the choice of lexical items that can be inserted into preterminal strings.

The transformational component mediates between the finite deep structure sentences and potentially infinite surface structure sentences and formally represents the structural relations between sentences. Whereas structural linguistics employs the taxonomic processes of segmentation and classification (or bracketing and labelling) to analyze the surface structure of language, TGG analyzes the more abstract rules underlying these sentences. In Chomsky's terminology, structural linguistics is only 'observationally adequate' (it is only able to describe a corpus of utterances), whereas the Standard Theory of TGG is 'descriptively adequate'. Within the context of a descriptively adequate theory of grammar, the formal

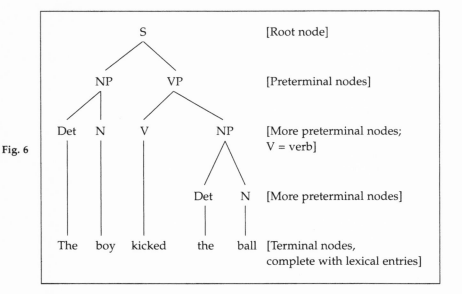

Fig. 6

rules constructed by the linguist represent the native speaker's competence, a point Chomsky emphasizes throughout his work: "On the basis of a limited experience with the data of speech, each normal human has developed for himself a thorough competence in his native language. This competence can be represented, to an as yet undetermined extent, as a system of rules that we can call the *grammar* of this language."[4] "A grammar can be regarded as a theory of a language; it is *descriptively adequate* to the extent that it correctly describes the intrinsic competence of the idealized native speaker. The structural descriptions assigned to sentences by the grammar, the distinctions that it makes between well formed and deviant, and so on, must, for descriptive adequacy, correspond to the linguistic intuition of the native speaker."[5] In a 1983 interview, he stated: "I would still want to resist what is a very common assumption, and I think one that is totally wrong, namely that the study of the abstract structure of language can't tell us anything about what is sometimes called 'psychological reality' or biological nature. On the contrary, it is precisely telling us about psychological reality in the only meaningful sense of that word."[6] Finally, Chomsky has recently written that "there can be little doubt that knowing a language involves internal representation of a generative procedure that specifies the structure of the language."[7] Ultimately, a descriptively adequate grammar like TGG is not justified by internal criteria of logical consistency, but must be adequate to a psychological reality. This position, known as 'mentalism,' advocates a strict identity (isomorphism) between theory and its object of study, the mental or cognitive reality external to it.

In a critical assessment of the cognitive status of Chomsky's linguistics, Scott Soames identifies two types of competence models and a performative model.[8] For Soames, the aim of a performance model "is to account for virtually all aspects of speaker judgment, sentence production, and sentence comprehension. This includes not only the nature and operation of internalized linguistic rules and strategies, but also the influence on linguistic behavior of non-linguistic cognitive systems such as those involving attention, perception, memory, and general ability to reason."[9] By contrast, "broadly construed" theories of linguistic competence (Soames's term) focus primarily on those aspects of the speaker-hearer's cognitive capacity involved in the mastery and use of language: "Their subject matter includes the speaker-hearer's internalized linguistic rules, plus any processing or heuristic procedures whose sole or primary applications are restricted to internal structures representing linguistic material."[10] Finally, Soames mentions theories of linguistic competence, narrowly construed: "These are theories of the speaker-hearer's internalized linguistic rules, minus any claims about the processing techniques or heuristics that determine how they are used."[11] Soames characterizes Chomsky's TGG as a theory of competence narrowly construed, that is, a highly idealized (cognitively unreal) theory. I shall return to Soames's characterization of Chomsky's theory in the final section of this chapter.

"The Grande Syntagmatique Revisited" (Michel Colin)

Colin's re-reading of Metz's *grande syntagmatique* (GS) consists of two steps: (1) a reconsideration of its formal properties in terms of the formal properties of the Standard Theory of TGG and (2) an attempt to determine its cognitive status.[12] The most striking aspect of Colin's writing is that it is exact (it aims to make explicit the implicit assumptions of Metz's film semiotics, and to follow them through to their logical conclusions), frequently fragmentary and detailed (it exhaustively deals with particular problems), and, more than any other film theory makes numerous references to specialized disciplines – not only TGG, but also other areas of cognitive science: artificial intelligence, philosophy of language, and computational linguistics. Thus his style and breadth of knowledge place great demands on the reader and make discussion of his work a long and arduous process. This explains the largely expositional nature of my discussion of his work, and the mainly technical nature of my criticisms.

For Colin, the GS consists of three types of 'object', which are related in terms of the three types of object in TGG: a root node (the autonomous segment), preterminal nodes (the six *classes* of syntagmas), and terminal nodes (the eight *types* of syntagmas). Colin begins his essay by representing Metz's formulation of the relation between these objects in terms of the tree diagram represented in Figure 7.

As in TGG, this tree diagram represents a series of re-write rules. The root node (autonomous segments) can be re-written as syntagmatic type 1, the autonomous shot, or the syntagmatic class of syntagmas. The class of syntagmas can be re-written as two other syntagmatic classes – achronological syntagmas and chronological syntagmas. Achronological syntagmas can be re-written as two syntagmatic types: 2, the parallel syntagma, and 3, the bracket syntagma, whereas the class of chronological syntagmas can be re-written as syntagmatic type 4, the descriptive syntagma, or the class of narrative syntagmas. The class of narrative syntagmas can be re-written as syntagmatic type 5, the alternate syntagma, or as the class of linear narrative syntagmas. The class of linear narrative syntagmas can be re-written as syntagmatic type 6, the scene, or as the class of sequences. Finally, the class of sequences can be re-written as two syntagmatic types: 7, the episodic sequence, and 8, the ordinary sequence.

The relations between the syntagmas can be represented by the following re-write rules:[13]

$$\text{Autonomous segments} \rightarrow \begin{bmatrix} \text{autonomous shot} \\ \text{syntagmas} \end{bmatrix}$$

$$\text{Syntagmas} \rightarrow \begin{bmatrix} \text{achronological syntagmas} \\ \text{chronological syntagmas} \end{bmatrix}, \text{etc.}$$

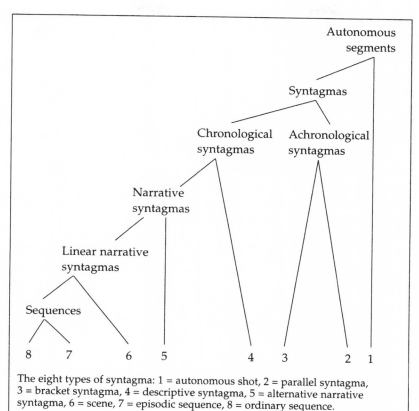

Fig. 7

The eight types of syntagma: 1 = autonomous shot, 2 = parallel syntagma, 3 = bracket syntagma, 4 = descriptive syntagma, 5 = alternative narrative syntagma, 6 = scene, 7 = episodic sequence, 8 = ordinary sequence.

Colin points out that whereas the tree diagrams and re-writing rules used in TGG represent a relation of conjunction, his tree diagram and re-writing rules represent a relation of disjunction. In other words, in TGG tree diagrams represent the syntactic relation between concatenated symbols, whereas in the GS the tree diagram represents alternative ways of re-writing the preterminal objects (the synatagmatic classes) – either as other syntagmatic classes or as terminal objects, the eight syntagmatic types. Moreover, in the GS the re-writing rules denote a relation of inclusion rather than concatenation. So the syntagmatic types 'episodic sequence' and 'ordinary sequence' are included within (are elements of) the syntagmatic class of sequences, which is itself included within the syntagmatic class of linear narrative syntagmas, and so on.

Colin goes on to emphasize the difference between a deductive reading and an inductive reading of the GS (a distinction introduced, but not elaborated, by Metz). A deductive (or top-down) reading of the GS considers it in terms of a series of re-writing rules, for we begin from an abstract root – autonomous segments – and continually re-write it until we reach the terminal objects, the actual syntagmatic types. An inductive (or bottom-up) reading starts from the syntagmatic types and defines them in terms of their specific characteristics (it spells out those features of syntagmatic types that make them identifiable). So an inductive reading considers each syntagmatic type in terms of its membership (relation of inclusion) to syntagmatic classes. Colin outlines these two types of reading in the following way: "The [relation of inclusion] depends, of course, on the direction in which the tree-diagram is being read, corresponding to what Metz calls an inductive method, starting from the syntagmatic types observed in the film (the terminal nodes). . . . Metz goes on to show another way of reading the tree, corresponding to what he calls the deductive method, starting from the root of the tree and progressing towards the terminal nodes."[14]

Later in the essay Colin formalizes in terms of selectional features the information obtained from both types of reading. But before he does this, he attempts to resolve some of the anomalies and asymmetries in the GS. For Colin, the dominant asymmetry of the GS is apparent from a deductive reading, which shows that, whereas most of the syntagmatic classes are re-written as a syntagmatic class and a syntagmatic type, the class of achronological syntagmas is re-written as two syntagmatic types (the parallel and bracket syntagmas), with no syntagmatic category (i.e., no defining characteristic) to distinguish them. (This information is manifest in the complete representation of the GS reproduced in Figure 7 and in Metz's table of the GS.[15]) Colin's aim is to make the GS completely symmetrical.[16]

For Metz, the bracket and parallel syntagmas are similar in that they present non-diegetic events, that is, shots of generic events inserted into the spatio-temporal order of the story world to illustrate a concept rather than to advance the story. Metz bases the distinction between the two syntagmas on the fact that the parallel syntagma consists of alternating shots of contrasting events (shots of the rich alternating with shots of the poor), whereas the bracket syntagma consists of a series of shots illustrating one concept, with the shots separated by optical devices. Metz gives the example of the beginning of Godard's *Une femme mariée* (1964), consisting of a series of erotic images illustrating the concept of 'modern love.'[17] Furthermore, for Metz, the generic characteristic of the parallel and bracket syntagmas is manifest in the fact that there are no spatio-temporal relations between the events depicted in them (both are therefore achronological).

But Colin argues that the surface structure characteristic of alternating images is insufficient to distinguish the two syntagmas and observes that if the optical devices are removed from the bracket syntagma, it can be read as a descriptive syntagma (the events can be read as diegetic and spatially co-existent). This leads Colin to emphasize the strong relation between the bracket and descriptive syntagmas, in which the only essential difference is the presence of optical effects in the bracket syntagma to deny a reading of spatial co-existence between the events depicted in each shot. Colin concludes that the bracket syntagma must be diegetic:

It may be seen that the possibility of confusion between the bracket and descriptive syntagmas implies that, unlike the parallel syntagma, the bracket syntagma is diegetic. The problem raised by Metz's table concerning the chronological/non-chronological distinction, which prevented any representation of the feature differentiating the bracket syntagma from the parallel syntagma, has thus been solved. The tree representation has become homogeneous: Each node is the starting point of two strings, one leading to a lower node, the other to a terminal node.[18]

Colin then produces a new, completely symmetrical tree diagram representing the core of the GS (see Figure 8).

This re-reading of Metz's GS permits Colin to represent the syntagmatic types in terms of selectional features, where each type is re-written as a set of specific traits:[19]

<pre>
    Parallel syntagma → <−diegetic, −linear>
     Bracket syntagma → <+diegetic, −specific>
 Descriptive syntagma → <+diegetic, +specific, −narrative,
                              +linear>
   Alternate syntagma → <+diegetic, +specific, +narrative,
                              −linear>
                Scene → <+diegetic, +specific, +narrative,
                              +linear, +inclusive>
             Sequence → <+diegetic, +specific, +narrative,
                              +linear, −inclusive>[20]
</pre>

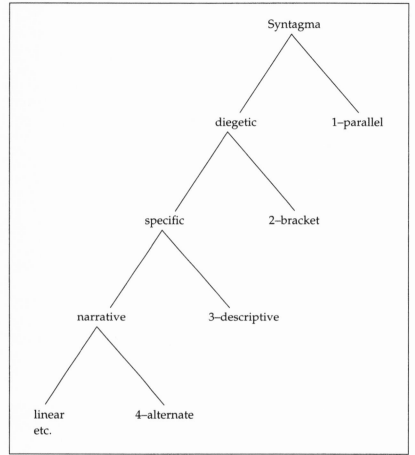

Fig. 8

Colin also proposes the following selectional features for the class 'Syntagma':[21]

(1)   Syntagma → <±syntagma, ±diegetic>
(2)   <+syntagma> → <±linear>
(3)   <+diegetic> → <±specific, ±narrative, ±inclusive>

Colin's use of these selectional features allows him to re-read the GS in a completely different way to other commentators. Early on he points out, "It must be said, first of all, that our purpose here is not, as it so often is with our discussions of the GS, to know whether or not Metz's list of syntagmatic types is a comprehensive one, whether it should be shortened or expanded. Our purpose is to determine what properties can help to define syntagmatic types, and what relationships exist between them."[22] As with all generative models, Colin's model does not merely describe existing syntagmatic types, but is also able to generate these existing syntagmatic types, together with possible/potential types and impossible types (a tripartite distinction familiar to linguistics, as we shall see ahead). This is probably one of the most innovative results of a generative re-reading of Metz's GS, and Colin begins to put this novel reading to work:

With the help of such rules, one can easily see that it is possible to deduce many more types than are represented in the table, for instance: a syntagma <+syntagma, +diegetic, −specific, −linear>, corresponds neither to the parallel syntagma (it is diegetic), nor to the alternate syntagma (it is not specific), although it has the same property as those two types (−linear). This, therefore, solves the problem of knowing how comprehensive the GS is, since it predicts the possibility of as yet undetected types. This, however, does not mean that everything is possible. The rules assume that certain types are impossible, for instance <−syntagma, −linear> [i.e., a non-linear sequence shot!].[23]

In the remainder of this chapter, I want to extend Colin's discussion of actual and non-actual syntagmatic types by using Chomsky's distinction between 'grammatical' and 'acceptable' sentences. More specifically, I would like to use this distinction to investigate grammatically deviant film syntagmas that spectators nonetheless judge to be acceptable or innovative, rather than simply confusing.

Generative Theories of Film Grammar

In 1974, at the First Congress of the International Association for Semiotic Studies (in Milan), Metz stated:

It is necessary to note that the work of film semiotics, in the vast majority of cases, is inspired more or less directly by models of structural or distributional linguistics, and not by generative linguistics. This is not by chance. ... Each film is an original product [un produit germiné], in the sense in which one does not find on the first approach grammatical nor ungrammatical sequences, but only attested combinations. In the midst of these filmic orderings that already exist, the first activity which attracts the analyst is that of calling attention to the regularities, co-occurrences, oppositions, recurrent 'motifs', progressions, etc., whose final synthesis constitutes a structural analysis. The generative semiotic perspective comes across an obstacle: the difficulty of defining in film a *criterion of grammaticality*.[24]

I want to argue that Metz's pessimism regarding the application of TGG to film was premature, because it is possible to define a criterion for filmic grammaticality.

In *Le cinéma comme langage*, Dominique Chateau has developed a transformational generative theory of film. At first, he seems skeptical about positing a theory of filmic 'competence' in Chomsky's sense of the word. Chateau notes that, for the most part, grammars developed by contemporary linguists are limited to the study of standard language, which represents the competence of a native speaker in an idealized situation of ordinary communication. But for Chateau, there are strong reasons against positing a standard cinematic language:

The most serious among them is incontestably . . . our incapacity to theoretically interpret the notion of a *series of ungrammatical filmic images*. A first advance by [Sol] Worth, then repeated by Metz, it is each time approached in relation to a discussion of the usefulness of the Chomskyan dichotomy competence/performance for the understanding of cinematic language.[25]

And

The deprivation of a standard cinematic language, due to the inadequacy in film of supposed ordinary communication, signifies that it is in vain to directly research a standard grammar for film, especially since the absence of a criterion of grammaticality does not allow . . . us to distinguish a subset of well-formed filmic segments.[26]

For Metz and Worth, because of the absence in film of a criterion of grammaticality, and therefore the absence of a standard cinematic language, it is implausible to posit a theory of filmic competence (a representation of the tacit knowledge directors/spectators possess that enables them to construct and comprehend filmic messages). On the other hand, Chateau believes that a study of cinematic language can nonetheless result in a plausible theory of filmic competence. This immediately leads to an apparent paradox in Chateau's position – but one he is well aware of. Stated bluntly, the paradox is, How can one reconcile the existence of filmic competence without positing the existence of a standard cinematic language and grammar? Chateau attempts to overcome this paradox by arguing that whereas natural language presupposes a number of strong principles regulating communication (principles that constitute the interlocutor's competence), in film the contract is based on much freer principles, to the point where the spectator will accept, as part of her tacit knowledge, new principles that are contradictory with those she already possesses. In other words, the principles that regulate cinematic language are variable, contingent, and continually open to revision. This is why throughout *Le cinéma comme langage* Chateau calls them "diverse rules of the game." Under these conditions, it is impossible, Chateau argues, to establish with any degree of certainty a standard cinematic language based on a stable grammar. But the "diverse rules of the game" still constitute the tacit knowledge directors/spectators need to possess to construct and understand films.

Chateau then notes that Metz's GS is prescriptive, since it refers to only one stylistic variation of cinematic language – 'classical' narrative cinema. Chateau characterizes this type of cinema as one overdetermined by the super-structural rule of narrative logic, and the GS as prescriptive because it represents this type of filmmaking as *the* language of film. In *Language and Cinema*, Metz attempts to counteract this imbalance by suggesting that the GS is merely a sub-code of the montage code. Without wishing to return to Metz's conflation, in "Problems of Denotation in the Fiction Film," of classical narrative film with cinematic language, I would still want to privilege the eight syntagmatic types identified by the GS as representing standard cinematic language (and its grammar) because of the reified status of these eight syntagmatic types. Furthermore, Chateau's positing of a lack of a standard cinematic language leads him to argue that it is impossible to identify semi-grammatical film sequences.[27] But my privileging of the GS as this standard will enable me to define semi-grammatical film sequences in cognitive terms. To do this, we need to return to Chomsky.

For Chomsky, a descriptively adequate grammar must be able to define 'degrees of grammaticalness', a phrase he defines as follows: "The degree of grammaticalness is a measure of the remoteness of an utterance from the generated set of perfectly well-formed sentences."[28] Jerrold J. Katz has expanded Chomsky's study of degrees of grammaticalness in his essay "Semi-Sentences"[29] (his term for semi-grammatical sentences). He raises the question of whether TGG (the primary aim of which is to generate all and only the sentences that native speakers judge to be well formed, or grammatical) can only explicate the speaker's knowledge of the structure of fully formed sentences, or whether it can also explicate the speaker's knowledge of semi-sentences. Within TGG, the speaker's understanding of a particular sentence is based upon her possessing the grammar that generated that sentence. By definition, this grammar only produces and comprehends (allows the speaker to comprehend) fully grammatical sentences. But clearly, Katz argues, speakers can understand semi-sentences as well. Katz then attempts to explain how speakers can comprehend semi-sentences. A semi-sentence contains elements of grammaticality and ungrammaticality (a sentence that is fully ungrammatical – or incomprehensible – is called by Katz a nonsense string). The main question, for Katz, "is what formal condition determines when a string has sufficient structure to be comprehensible"[30] (a formal condition that enables the analyst to distinguish semi-sentences from nonsense strings). His answer involves the speaker's applying rules of association between fully grammatical sentences and semi-sentences: "A speaker knows (in the sense in which he knows the rules of the grammar of his language) a system of rules that enables him to associate a non-null set of grammatical sentences with each semi-sentence. This association is performed on the basis of the structure that the semi-sentence has. And the speaker's understanding of the semi-sentence is nothing other than his understanding of the sentences in the set with which the semi-sentence is associated."[31] For Katz, therefore, the semi-sentence, to be comprehended, must possess sufficient grammatical structure that it can be associated with a fully grammatical sentence.

In *Aspects of the Theory of Syntax*, Chomsky stresses that well-formedness/grammaticality does not wholly determine acceptability: "Acceptability is a concept that belongs to the study of performance, whereas grammaticalness belongs to the study of competence. . . . Grammaticalness is only one of many factors that interact to determine acceptability."[32] Constraints on acceptability include memory limitation and intonational factors. Keeping in mind the interdependence of grammar and acceptability, we can employ the well-known tripartite distinction between actual, possible/potential, and impossible sequences to distinguish between linguistic and filmic constructions that are grammatical and acceptable, ungrammatical but acceptable, and ungrammatical and unacceptable (see Figure 9).

	Phonology	Grammar	Narrative fiction film
1. Actual	'pet'	'a year ago'	the 8 syntagmatic types
2. Possible/ potential	'lon'	'a grief ago'	Metz's example from Godard (see text)
3. Impossible	'atp'	'a the ago'	non-linear sequence shot

Fig. 9

Category 1 refers to grammatical and acceptable sequences, 2 to ungrammatical but acceptable, and 3 to ungrammatical and unacceptable sequences. A linguistic construction can also be grammatical and unacceptable, insofar as it is produced by the generative and transformational rules of the grammar but it overstretches certain faculties of performance such as memory. This applies to very long sentences (produced by the recursive application of a particular transformational rule, for example) or to sentences containing multiply embedded structures. An open question is whether a filmic sequence can be grammatical and unacceptable.

In Figure 9, category 1, of course, is from everyday discourse (all the grammatical examples are taken from Chomsky). The eight actual film syntagmas outlined in the GS define grammatical and acceptable film sequences, which constitute the hypothetical norm of narrative film sequencing, as embodied in classical Hollywood films. Here I am using the term 'grammatical' in Chomsky's technical sense (discussed previously), which allows us to describe the eight syntagmatic categories as grammatical in that they denote sequences generated by the filmic re-write rules and are therefore recognized by competent film spectators as being well formed.

Category 2 defines semi-sentences, together with those sequences that are possible according to the rules of grammar (i.e., like those in category 1 they are regular sequences) but that, for accidental, historical, and/or psychological reasons, have not been employed in everyday discourse. (Chomsky's syntactic example is from Dylan Thomas's poetry, although examples from Lewis Carroll's nonsense verse or from Joyce's *Finnegan's Wake*, for example, also belong to this category.) Metz makes a passing reference to possible/potential constructions in the cinema in his essay "Modern Cinema and Narrativity,"[33] in which he rejects the common assumption that the 'modern' (i.e., the French New Wave) cinema rejected narrative. Instead, he argues that it adopts a new type of narrativity:

Far from demonstrating the nonexistence of "syntax," [the French New Wave directors] are really discovering new syntactic regions while remaining (at least as long as they are intelligible, as is the case almost always) entirely submissive to the functional requirements of filmic discourse. *Alphaville* and *Last Year in Marienbad* are still, from one end to the other, diegetic films, and they were still conceived in relation to the requirements of narrative fiction, despite their undoubted originality, their editing, and their montage.[34]

Except for the comment in parentheses, Metz is referring to the formal dimension of French New Wave films. But immediately he adds a cognitive dimension to his argument (or extends the preceding cognitive statement in parentheses):

Impossible constructions do exist in the cinema. . . . But such orderings have never been seriously tried by film-makers, unless perhaps – and even then one would have to examine the matter more closely – by some extreme avant-gardist who had deliberately abandoned the effort to make himself understood (and, then, usually in cinematographic "genres" initially foreign to the narrative fiction film). And the reason that the other film-makers never attempt to construct such combinations, or even to imagine that they might exist, is precisely because *the main figures of cinematographic intelligibility inhabit their minds* [emphasis added] to a much greater extent than they are aware of.[35]

Clearly, in the terminology I established in Figure 9, Metz means 'possible' or 'potential' rather than 'impossible' constructions (and later in the essay, he uses the term 'potential'). The main point of this passage, however, is Metz's insistence that the French New Wave directors challenged the norms that constitute conventional cinematic intelligibility, epitomized in classical Hollywood cinema. This is not surprising from directors brought up on Hollywood films who nonetheless attempted to produce their own distinctive style.

As an example of a possible/potential construction, Metz cites the sequence from Godard's *Pierrot le fou* in which the two protagonists, Pierrot and Marianne, hurriedly leave Marianne's apartment. This sequence juxtaposes shots of the protagonists escaping from the apartment with shots of the protagonists several minutes into their journey. After rejecting a classification of this sequence in terms of his eight syntagmatic types, Metz concludes:

In the midst of the frenzy of the hasty departure ([signified] of the denotation), it presents as equal possibilities – which implies a sort of self-confession to narrativity, an awareness of its own fablic nature – several *slightly* different variations of a frantic escape, sufficiently similar to each other nevertheless for the event that really did occur (and which we will never know) to take place among a class of quite clearly outlined occurrences. . . . [Godard] is able to suggest with a great deal of truth, but without determining the outcome, several possibilities at the same time. So he gives us a sort of *potential sequence* – an undetermined sequence – that represents a new type of syntagma, a novel form of the "logic of montage," *but that remains entirely a figure of narrativity.*[36]

I shall briefly discuss category 3 before returning to this example. Category 3 of Figure 9 illustrates irregular sequences that violate phonemic, syntactic, and filmic rules of sequencing. These sequences are called impossible because the phonemic sequence cannot be pronounced, the syntactic sequence cannot be processed by the speaker (i.e., given a semantic interpretation), and the filmic sequence cannot be produced (as Colin argued).

Category 2 is the most interesting in filmic terms (and, indeed, in linguistic terms), for it expresses a complex relation between structure, cognition, and aesthetics. What makes such grammatically deviant sequences acceptable is that their remoteness from well-formed sequences can be measured, or calculated by the speaker. Chomsky writes: "Given a grammatically deviant utterance, we attempt to impose an interpretation on it, exploiting whatever features of grammatical structure it preserves and whatever analogies we can construct with perfectly well-formed utterances."[37] In filmic and linguistic terms, category 1 requires the 'standard' (or 'optimally relevant') amount of processing to construct a semantic comprehension, whereas category 2 requires an additional amount of processing effort to yield a semantic interpretation (usually accompanied by an aesthetic payoff). The examples in category 3 will not yield to any semantic comprehension because they do not preserve any grammatical features.

In *Pierrot le fou*, the characters' escape is comprehensible because it is possible for spectators to relate, using what Katz calls the 'rules of association', this semi-sequence to a fully grammatical sequence. This challenges Metz's suggestion that the spectator will never know the actual event that did occur.

This process of reading a potential sequence of film within the context of actual filmic sequences has been partially formalized by

Chateau. In a discussion of Metz's analysis of the sequence in *Pierrot le fou*, Chateau argues that the director dismantles a well-formed sequence and then rearranges the shots into a new order, to express the characters' sense of panic and haste. Similarly, the spectator must attempt to reconstruct the linear order that has been disrupted, in order to grasp the meaning of the sequence. Chateau seems to argue that this particular sequence from *Pierrot le fou* is an ordinary sequence (in Metz's sense of the term) that has undergone a transformation. Although Chateau does not pursue this issue any further, it is possible to explain this transformation by referring to Chomsky's trace theory. And the best way to explain the trace theory is by means of the derivational history of the following sentence:

(1a) John was expected [John to hurt himself]
(1b) John was expected [t to hurt himself]
(1c) John was expected to hurt himself

(1a) is a deep structure sentence made up of two clauses. Both clauses contain the same subject ('John'). For this deep structure to yield a grammatical surface structure sentence, the subject of the embedded clause (the embedded clause is in parentheses) must be deleted, yielding sentence (1c). Although the second subject has been deleted, it still leaves a trace in the deep structure of the sentence, sentence (1b). But why must it leave a trace? For Chomsky, the trace represents an important piece of information in the competent speaker's mental representation of the surface structure sentence: "The trace t, though not pronounced, is actually present in the mental representation of the sentence. It is 'seen' by the mind as the mind computes the structure of the sentence . . . but it is not pronounced by the vocal mechanisms because it contains no phonetic features."[38] The trace is an empty category, but it functions in the same way as the proper noun it has replaced (the trace possesses the same syntactic and semantic properties as the category it has replaced).

What is important for my argument here is that in the sentence 'John was expected to hurt himself', 'John' is *understood* to be the subject of the verb 'hurt' as well as the subject of the verb 'expect'. The deep structure trace (which has no surface structure representation) represents the competent speaker's underlying knowledge that 'John' is the subject of the verb 'hurt'.

The sequence from *Pierrot le fou* is an ungrammatical but acceptable filmic sequence. It is acceptable because it can be associated with a grammatical sequence. Or, in the terms just used, it can be *understood* in relation to a grammatical sequence.

I shall attempt to reconstruct this sequence by putting its shots (back) into a grammatical sequence. The sequence contains fourteen shots, each of which corresponds to fourteen events. The following description outlines the fourteen shots as they present the order of events in the film.

Shot No.	*Events*
1.	Marianne (Anna Karina) and Pierrot (Jean Paul Belmondo) in Marianne's apartment. Frank (Marianne's lover) enters and is ambushed by Marianne and Pierrot. Marianne prepares to leave the apartment, and Pierrot begins to drag Frank away.
2.	Marianne driving a red car. Pierrot gets in.
3.	Marianne and Pierrot exit the bathroom (Frank, unconscious, has been put in the bath).
4.	The red car is seen speeding along a street. It drives under a height restriction barrier.
5.	Marianne and Pierrot on the apartment roof. They look down. Cut to:
6.	Two men running toward the apartment.
7.	Cut back to Marianne and Pierrot on the roof (continuation of 5).
8.	Cut to Marianne and Pierrot climbing down a drain pipe.
9.	Repetition of shot 2 (slightly truncated).
10.	The red car driving along a street. The height restriction barrier can be seen ahead in the distance.
11.	Marianne gets into the red car and drives off.
12.	The car approaches the height restriction barrier.
13.	Point of view shot from the car wind screen of a replica of the Statue of Liberty. The height restriction barrier is briefly seen in the shot.
14.	The red car pulls up at a petrol station.

Each action can be assigned a letter to illustrate the disjunction between shot number and event order:

Actual sequence

Shot number: 1 2 3 4 5 6 7 8 9 10 11 12 13 14

Order of events: a h b k c d e f h i g j l m

The shots can be re-arranged to conform to an ordinary sequence (can be associated with an ordinary sequence):

Re-arranged order of sequence

1 3 5 6 7 8 11 2/9 10 12 4 13 14

a b c d e f g   h i j k l m

In terms of the events depicted, we can divide the sequence into two: events a–g (escape from the apartment) and events h–m (both protagonists driving away). In the actual sequence, three events (g, h, and k) have been displaced and re-inserted into the sequence. But this only makes five displaced events (rather than six) because event h (Pierrot getting into the car) has been duplicated before being displaced. In terms of the sequence's linear narrative order, the progression from a to b (the ambush of Frank and placing him in the bath) has been interrupted by h (Pierrot getting into the car), and the progression from b to c (Marianne and Pierrot exiting the bathroom and going onto the roof of the apartment) has been interrupted by k (the car driving under the height restriction barrier). The progression from c to f (Pierrot and Marianne on the roof of the apartment, seeing the men below, and climbing down a drain pipe) remains intact. Event g (Marianne getting into the car) has been displaced two shots forward. Events h and i (Pierrot getting into the car and driving along the street) remain intact. The progression from i to j (the car approaching the height restriction barrier) is interrupted by g (Marianne getting into the car). The car going under the barrier (k) has been displaced into the first half of the sequence, between b and c (Marianne and Pierrot exiting the bathroom and going onto the roof of the apartment).

What this analysis reveals is that two events from the second half of the sequence (h, Pierrot getting into the car, and k, the car going under the height restriction barrier) have been displaced into the first half of the sequence, whereas one event in the first half (g, Marianne getting into the car) has been displaced into the second half of the sequence.

It is possible to assign letters to the events depicted in each shot and reconstruct the sequence because the original position of the events and shots is (in Chomsky's terms) marked by a trace. A trace contains the same syntactic and semantic features as the shots/ event it replaces. In a shot, as Metz's GS emphasizes, these features include spatio-temporal coordinates, together with the cause-effect narrative logic linking the events. In terms of h (the repeated shot of Pierrot getting into the car), it is possible to argue that its original position is shot 9, but that it has been displaced to shot 2. Moreover, it has not left a trace, but has been duplicated before being displaced. Hence, whereas the other displacements cause two disruptions (their old location and their new location), this duplication creates only one disturbance (the new location).

This process of reconstruction shows that the sequence can be understood by the spectator: The spectator 'understands' that shot 2, for example (Pierrot getting into the car), jumps ahead to show future events (in shot 1 Pierrot is shown dragging the unconscious Frank, whereas in shot 2 Pierrot is getting into a car; such a jump depicts spatio-temporal as well as narrative displacement). Such an understanding would not be possible if shot 2 depicted a deep sea diver searching for buried treasure, for example. I am therefore arguing that the re-constructed ordinary sequence is 'present' in the spectator's mental representation of the sequence – present not in its pure form, of course, but in the sequence's actual form together with traces. And it is from these traces that the ordinary sequence can be re-constructed. When seen at the cinema, the grammar of this sequence conveys the confusion of the protagonists' escape. But the grammar does not arrange the shots haphazardly (they do not result in a nonsense string of shots). Instead, it still has a structure, which can be associated with a fully grammatical structure (as represented in the GS).

Chateau's claim that this sequence from *Pierrot le fou* represents the re-writing of a grammatical filmic sequence has two effects: (1) It challenges Metz's reading of the sequence, in which he states that it represents "several *slightly* different variations of a frantic escape, sufficiently similar to each other nevertheless for the event that really did occur (and which we will never know)."[39] Contrary to Metz's reading, the sequence presents only one variation of the escape, which, when re-constructed, can be known by the spectators. (2) Secondly, Chateau's re-reading of this sequence reinforces

my argument that the GS can be taken to represent a standard
grammar of film, one that generates well-formed sequences, and in
relation to which deviant (or semi-) syntagmas can be comprehended. We saw that for Chomsky and Jerrold J. Katz semi-
sentences are comprehensible according to their association with
fully grammatical sentences (the remoteness of semi-sentences from
well-formed sentences can be measured, or calculated by the
speaker). In analogous fashion, I am claiming that 'semi-syntagmas'
(or deviant syntagmas) are those that can be associated with one or
more of the eight syntagmatic types of the GS. If no association is
possible, then the collection of shots must be categorized as a nonsense string. The fully grammatical syntagmas of the GS are defined
and distinguished according to their spatio-temporal coordinates
(which represent the film's diegesis in a coherent, or comprehensible, manner). Deviation is calculable in terms of an ungrammatical
syntagma's difference from the spatio-temporal relations represented in the fully grammatical syntagmas of the GS. As long as
that difference is measurable (as it is in the sequence from *Pierrot le
fou*), then the syntagma can still be comprehended.

But we can go further than Chomsky's and Katz's discussions
of the degrees of grammaticalness. The GS constitutes well-formed,
or grammatical, film sequences, not so much because of any formal
criteria they may conform to, but because its eight syntagmas constitute the hypothetical norm of narrative film processing, or comprehension. Ill-formed (ungrammatical) syntagmas require from
the spectator an additional amount of processing effort. Although
Metz defines the syntagmas in formal terms, it seems to me that
they conform to Sperber and Wilson's cognitive principle of relevance.

The spectator's processing of narrative film is governed by the
goal of constructing a coherent literal meaning – or a coherent
narrative world (diegesis). As David Bordwell argues, the film's
fabula (a concept that parallels the concept of the diegesis) is inherently fragmentary and must be completed by the cognitive activity
of the spectator. In Metz's film semiotics, the eight categories of the
GS are constructed according to the principle of relevance – they
are the optimal shot orderings, for they permit the spectator to
employ the least amount of processing effort while yielding an
optimal contextual effect (= the spectator's construction of a diegesis). Ill-formed syntagmas thwart the principle of relevance, be-

cause they require additional processing effort from the spectator in order to construct/comprehend a coherent narrative world. However, if this additional processing effort is successful, it results in an aesthetic pay-off (which explains the select audience for the international art cinema and its corresponding characterization as aesthetic). But if this additional processing effort is unsuccessful, it may simply lead to boredom and confusion (hence the international art cinema is not inherently aesthetic; its aesthetic effects are partly achieved from the mental effort – or, more formally, competence – of the spectator).

We can now apply the principle of relevance to the three categories outlined. In category 1, actual sequences, the principle of relevance operates automatically. In category 2, potential sequences, it operates with conscious effort (and this additional effort is usually rewarded by an aesthetic pay-off). But in category 3, impossible sequences, the principle of relevance does not operate, leading to incomprehension.

What exactly are the increased processing effort and aesthetic pay-off in category 2 sequences? Firstly, the spectator must work harder to construct a coherent diegesis – must work harder simply to determine what is happening in the film. We have already seen this in relation to *Pierrot le fou*. A further example is given by David Bordwell in *Narration in the Fiction Film*, in an analysis of Alain Resnais'a film *La Guerre est finie* (1968).[40] Bordwell concentrates on the first nineteen shots of the film. It begins with Diego (a left-wing political agitator) driving back across the Spanish-French border with his collaborator Jude. A number of the shots are overlaid with a non-diegetic voice-over expressing Diego's anxieties about crossing the border. This is followed by Jude speaking off-screen. As he does so, the spectator sees nine shots depicting Diego performing a number of actions (catching a cab, meeting his friend Juan, missing his friend Juan, waiting for a cab, walking down a train corridor, catching a train, missing a train, and being greeted by Juan). Bordwell writes that "the mode of presentation [of these nine shots] must give the spectator pause. Seeing that shots 9–17 rupture the spatiotemporal continuum of the scene in the car and hearing Jude's chatter continuing in voice-over, the viewer versed in the convention of the art cinema hypothesizes a temporal disjunction between sound (the present) and image (not the present). But the ambiguities of the sequence thwart any easy comprehension."[41] Translated into Sperber and Wilson's terms, what Bordwell means here, in effect, is that this sequence of nine shots cannot be automatically processed (i.e., processed in accordance with the principle of relevance). As with the sequence from *Pierrot le fou*, this sequence cannot be categorized in terms of any of the eight syntagmatic types represented in Metz's GS. The nine shots do not, therefore, represent a fully grammatical sequence.

Bordwell then goes on to explore whether the sequence can be comprehended at all. He notes that the shots cannot be comprehended as presenting a single event chain; rather, they represent mutually exclusive alternatives – Diego catches/does not catch a cab quickly; Diego calls on Juan/misses Juan/Diego calls and Juan arrives later; Diego catches/does not catch the train (it is this structure of mutually exclusive alternative events that Metz wrongly attributed to *Pierrot le fou*). Bordwell then ponders whether the shots represent past actions, frequentative actions (depicting Diego's regular routine), or future actions. Although the least likely the last hypothesis, Bordwell argues, is the only one that can sufficiently explain/motivate these shots: "Only one construction accounts for everything in these shots. It is an unlikely one, but it is the one that later passages will confirm. These shots may be taken to represent various possible future events. Put in simple fashion: 'I might grab a cab right away or have to wait in line,' 'I might miss Juan,' 'what if I can't catch a train?' *La Guerre est finie* will explore character subjectivity according to one principle of the art film; we justify what we see and hear by reference to psychological motivation."[42] That the shots represent future events is not an inference automatically generated by the spectator when watching the film. The spectator must work harder than normal to find the optimally relevant inference – the one that will motivate these nine shots. Like all non-demonstrative inferences, the one claiming that the shots are of future events is open to revision. However, as Bordwell notes, this inference is strengthened by later sequences.

The spectator's additional processing effort involved in comprehending semi-syntagmas leads not only to the construction of a coherent diegesis, but also to the construction of an auteur who has manipulated the shots for aesthetic effect. (In Roger Odin's terms, semi-syntagmas are prominent in the artistic mode of filmmaking, since the film is read as the product of an auteur.) For Bordwell, on the one hand, art cinema narration is based on objective and expressive realism. On the other hand, it is highly self-conscious, as a result of the flaunting of narrational procedures. Bordwell writes that "when these flauntings are repeated systematically, conventions ask us to unify them as proceeding from an author."[43] Although Bordwell rejects the communicational model of film – particularly its emphasis on the 'sender' of a message (see Chapter 2) – he argues that the positing of an author is necessary in Resnais's film: "The average spectator of *La Guerre est finie* (1968) is likely to approach the film with some expectations about the principal narrational manipulations the film will offer and to attribute those to an authorial intelligence."[44]

In discussing *Pierrot le fou* and *La Guerre est finie*, I have begun to define the boundaries between grammatical (and acceptable), ungrammatical (but acceptable), and ungrammatical (and unacceptable) film sequences, a definition not based purely on formal criteria but also on cognitive criteria (how spectators comprehend grammatical and deviant syntagmas). One conclusion we can reach is that there is a marked difference in processing effort between 'classical' narrative films (whose syntagmas conform to the hypothetical norm outlined in Metz's GS) and films identified as belonging to the avant-garde or to international art cinema (whose syntagmas deviate from those in the GS). Correlatively, classical films conform to the principle of relevance (the hypothetical norm of processing activity), whereas films of the international art cinema deviate from the principle of relevance, since they require additional processing effort, which is usually rewarded with an aesthetic pay-off.

However, we should not conclude that spectators automatically abide by the principle of relevance in comprehending films. This principle simply expresses a rational norm, from which actual groups of spectators may deliberately prefer to deviate. The increase in processing effort may not simply be demanded by the filmic text, but may be instigated by the spectator. This is precisely the conclusion that Lerdahl and Jackendoff reach in their generative theory of tonal music. They find that the specificity of music cannot simply be described in terms of grammatical rules, but also requires a series of what they call preference rules:

We have found that a generative music theory, unlike a generative linguistic theory, must not only assign structural descriptions to a piece, but must also differentiate them along a scale of coherence, weighting them as more or less "preferred" interpretations (that is, claimimg that the experienced listener is more likely to attribute some structures to the music than others). Thus the rules of the theory are divided into two distinct types: *well-formedness* [i.e., grammatical] rules, which specify the possible structural descriptions, and *preference rules*, which designate out of possible structural descriptions those that correspond to experienced listeners' hearings of any particular piece.[45]

Preference rules therefore represent a series of alternative, but plausible, structural descriptions of a piece of text. Whereas sentences of natural language (except ambiguous sentences) are subject to one unique structural description, music, Lerdahl and Jackendoff argue, does not demand a singular grammatical description, but a series of preference rules.

Such preference rules very likely operate in the comprehension of films as well because, as Dominique Chateau makes clear, there is no highly formalized grammar of the cinema to demand a singular grammatical description. This means that, under specific circumstances, the comprehension of a film may be governed by preference rules, of which the principle of relevance is only one (although the dominant one). This can then explain how cinephiles can identify authorial structures in 'classical' Hollywood films – they prefer to select different cues and experience a different structure than non-cinephiles. To read a Hollywood film for its authorial structures, rather than simply for its literal meaning, is a non-relevance-determined strategy preferred by cinephiles. We can draw an analogy with the choice readers face when confronted with an ironic or allegorical text. Some readers may interpret the text literally, whereas others are able to comprehend it figuratively.

With their theory of preference rules, Lerdahl and Jackendoff restate the principle of relevance as follows: "Prefer to assume that the speaker is conveying something relevant."[46] As a preference rule, the principle of relevance should not be taken to represent the necessary and sufficient conditions for all film spectators in comprehending a film, but to represent one preferred way among many – although admittedly it governs the most basic and literal level of comprehension. Unlike the idealized 'normal' spectator, cinephiles prefer to go beyond the principle of relevance to concentrate on what the filmmaker is not conveying directly.

We can therefore posit that film has a special (or rather 'loose') type of grammar: For Chateau, for example, the grammar of film is based on "diverse rules of the game"; or we can say that it is no more than a preference rule (reflecting the inherent ambiguity of filmic structure, as with tonal music); or we can say that it is based on the pragmatic (therefore defeasible) principle of relevance. For Metz, the grammar of film is inseparable from rhetoric: "The nature of the semiotics of film is that grammar and rhetoric are not separate in it."[47] Metz refers specifically to the classical rhetorical trope of *dispositio*, which consists of "prescribing determined orderings to undetermined elements."[48] Whereas shots are undetermined, their ordering does pertain to a degree of determination, and the semiotic analysis of the grammar of film attempts to discover both its nature and its degree of determination. The trace theory and preference rules have been introduced in this chapter to outline a number of cognitive determinations of film. These two cognitive rules, together with the principle of relevance, complement the distinctions made in this chapter, among actual, possible (potential), and impossible filmic sequences, and go some way to predicting why those sequences identified by the GS are frequently employed in narrative films, why semi-sequences are rarely employed, and why others not employed at all. These predictions in turn confirm the cognitive reality of filmic sequences as analyzed by the cognitive film semioticians, for they suggest that frequently used sequences are more easily comprehended than difficult sequences, and some sequences are not employed at all because spectators cannot process them.

Film Semiotics and Cognitive Science

Chomsky favored grammars that captured ... "linguistically significant generalizations" [Chomsky, *Aspects*, 42] but the question that immediately struck many psychologists was whether linguistically significant generalizations were also psychologically significant.[49]

Within the context of TGG, film semiotics is characterized as positing a relation of identity between its semiotic descriptions and cognitively real structures, namely, cognitive states and processing operations in the spectator's mind. We need to follow the cognitive interpretations of Colin to answer the following question: What are the reasons for making cognitive claims about film semiotics? One immediate answer suggests itself – to increase the power of film semiotics, that is, to make it descriptively adequate rather than merely observationally adequate. Whether a descriptively adequate

theory of film semiotics is an improvement on Metz's observationally adequate theory is a question I shall begin to answer in the
following pages.

In the conclusion to "The Grande Syntagmatique Revisited"
Colin makes two contradictory assertions concerning the cognitive
reality of Metz's GS. Colin stresses throughout his essay that the
primary motivation for his re-reading of the GS is pedagogic – how
can it be taught? It is in answer to this question that he at first
asserts the cognitive *un*reality of the GS: "It thus seems quite reasonable to use segmentation as a starting point when teaching the
GS. This, however, does not imply that spectatorial competence
proceeds in the same way. It is even conceivable that an explicit
theory on this competence would not have to distinguish between
these two procedures."[50] But on the next page, after briefly considering the function of sound in the analysis of film, Colin asserts:
"In this sense, there is no reason to distinguish between 'image
track' and 'sound track', since the GS can be considered as an
explicit analysis of syntagmatic relationships between the mental
images constructed by the spectator on the basis of the visual and
acoustic information provided by the film."[51] Here, Colin confers
on the GS a cognitive reality, suggesting that it is a descriptively
adequate theory, a theory of the film spectator's underlying competence.

Like the TG grammarians, Colin is arguing that a TGG-based
film semiotics does not merely offer a formal way of generating
and representing filmic structures, but also represents cognitively
real structures in the spectator (in other words, the formal filmic
structures explained by the semiotician are cognitive representations). Again, as with the TG grammarians, Colin is equating formal
rules of grammar with cognitive states.

In an essay already cited, Scott Soames (among many others)
argues that grammars (grammatical rules) and theories of competence are independent of one another. Whereas grammars characterize languages as formal systems of symbol manipulation, theories of competence attempt to uncover cognitive structures, which
cannot be characterized simply or primarily in terms of formal
systems of symbol manipulation, for linguistic cognitive structures
involve far more than a narrowly construed notion of competence.
Soames is following many researchers in artificial intelligence in
making a strong distinction between linguistics and cognitive psy-

chology, for he denies that grammar is cognitively real (i.e., he denies it plays a role in language processing). He offers two straightforward reasons: "There are linguistic facts which are not psychological in nature," and "There are psychological facts which are non-linguistic."[52] Here Soames is rehearsing the modular theory of the mind, which posits that the mind consists of separate information processing devices, each geared to the processing of particular types of information. By contrast, the non-modular view models the processing of *all* information in terms of one general cognitive apparatus. Because of the richness and complexity of natural language, it is regarded to constitute the general cognitive apparatus.

But we do not need to adopt a fully modular theory of the mind to avoid the 'translinguistics' of semiotics and structuralism, or to deny that grammar plays a role in the processing of language. A number of grammarians have argued that the Standard Theory of TGG was simply the wrong theory. Thomas G. Bever notes that three trends developed during the 1980s in an attempt to renew the relation between linguistics and psychology: (1) Chomsky's Government and Binding theory; (2) Joan Bresnan's lexical-functional grammar; and (3) the Generalized Phrase Structure Grammar of Gerald Gazdar.[53] All three models are notable for having greatly reduced (or abandoned completely) the transformational component of grammar.

In a review of Metz's *Film Language,* John M. Carroll takes a different approach to Colin in assessing the cognitive status of film semiotics. Carroll writes: "The categories and binary features of the grande syntagmatique are not aspects of consciousness in film viewing. They are theoretical entities, aspects of a model, and constitute a break with experience. Of course, if the taxonomy has any efficacy, it will ultimately be relevant to models of conscious experience."[54] Here Carroll indicates the cognitive unreality of the GS but also stresses that a formal model of film becomes a satisfying theory only to the extent that it has cognitive implications. Later in the review, he makes a tentative suggestion:

It would be odd indeed if any purely formal analysis of film turned out to be psychologically significant independent of general facts about human perception. If the film theory includes the facts about perception in its own statements, we risk confusing generalizations about perception with generalizations about film structure. A more reasonable hypothesis is that a formal analysis of film becomes psychologically significant through the interaction with various behavioral systems (e.g. perception).[55]

In *Toward a Structural Psychology of Cinema*,[56] Carroll attempts, less successfully than Colin, to develop a TGG of film and to theorize the interactions of film structure, perception, and aesthetics. He argues that an aesthetic theory of filmic perception must be based on a formal model and proposes that TGG can offer the most explicit formal model of film, hence can serve as the most adequate framework for an aesthetic theory of film. The most important question that such an aesthetic theory must confront is, "How do grammar and aesthetic theory interact, how do they relate to each other in the integrated theory?"[57] Carroll stresses that grammar cannot by itself determine the aesthetic value of a filmic (or linguistic) sequence, for it is an aesthetically neutral theory of cognition. He then feels justified to distinguish the 'filmic' and the 'cinematic': "The term 'filmic' will be used to refer to sequences which are structurally correct and therefore well-formed . . . the term 'cinematic' will hereafter be used to refer to cinema sequences that are artistically and stylistically valuable."[58] A 'filmic' sequence according to Carroll is one that obeys the rules of filmmaking (obeys the 180 and 30 degree rules, constructs readable point of view sequences, maintains an unambiguous relation between the space of each shot and the space of the sequence it forms part of, etc.), whereas a 'cinematic' film is structurally incorrect and ill formed. Although Carroll notes that these terms do not correspond to aesthetic judgements, he nonetheless implies that 'filmic' means routine and pedestrian, and 'cinematic' means artistically valuable (precisely the term he uses to define the 'cinematic').

In a programmatic essay, Carroll cites several examples of 'cinematic' sequences (all based on confusing spatial relations). Here I shall cite one of his examples:

In Hitchcock's *Psycho* while the detective climbs the stairs (just before he is murdered), there is a cut to the base of a door just beginning to open (as we later find out, the bedroom door). Where the door is, the viewer does not know at the time of the cut.

. . . . It is very clear that Hitchcock, for example, *wanted* the geography of the door to be unspecified – this unclarity is the basis for the suspense of the sequence. . . . This [unclarity] is quite irrelevant to a formal *model* of film but crucial to an *aesthetic*. . . . The sequences we have just discussed are unacceptable but they may all be very successful aesthetically.[59]

Moreover, in his book Carroll defines 'aesthetically pleasing' in terms of a theory of tension (in which the value of art is located in the conflicts it creates). According to Carroll, tension is created in film through a conflict between event/action boundaries and shot boundaries. In his own TGG-based theory of film (outlined in the central chapters of *Toward a Structural Psychology of Cinema*), Carroll conceives the base component as a device that generates events, each consisting of a series of actions (some of which can be optionally re-written as preparatory and focal sub-actions).[60] Each action is represented in the form of a proposition. Furthermore, the boundary between two or more propositions (actions) represents a major constituent boundary (the boundary between preparatory and focal actions represents a minor constituent boundary). Transformational rules then transform these actions into filmic sequences. The most important rule involves representing the actions in a sequence of shots (or placing cuts within the chain of actions and sub-actions). The relation between action boundaries and shot boundaries allows Carroll to develop a theory of motivated and unmotivated cutting, as follows: "If a cut coincides with a major boundary, the cut is motivated by the event. If the cut coincides with a minor boundary, the cut is motivated by an action in the event. If a cut coincides with a nonboundary, it is not motivated."[61] For Carroll, tension in the cinema occurs when shot boundaries do not coincide with action/event boundaries. Carroll establishes five different sequence structures for the same event structure – that is, devises five different ways of placing cuts within a sequence consisting of three actions.[62] Zero tension is created when shot boundaries coincide with action boundaries, and maximum tension is created when there is little or no coincidence.

Carroll develops a very simplistic, almost quantitative, theory of aesthetics based on a formal model. The less coincidence between action and shot boundaries, the more tension and so the more aesthetic pleasure created by the sequence. The arithmetic is elegant but hardly bears up to scrutiny. For example, one tension-creating sequence consists of the three actions being filmed in one shot! There is certainly no coincidence between action boundaries and shot boundaries (at least within the sequence); according to Carroll, therefore, it must create a great deal of tension. But this conclusion fails to take into account the structure within the image – that is, camera movements, and so on (for a camera movement can be functionally equivalent to a cut); nor does it consider the arbitrary division of filmic events into action, sub-actions, and so on. Carroll seems to uphold the classical film theorists' distinction between montage and the long take, in which the two devices are distinguished according to their materiality, not their function.

My extension of Colin's work on actual and non-actual syntagmatic types (through the introduction of the work of Chomsky and Katz on semi-sentences) makes a tentative link between grammatical structure, cognitive processing effort, and aesthetics, indicating that structure does at least have a partial cognitive reality. However, unlike the early psycholinguists, I do not propose an isomorphic relation between structural complexity and processing complexity. The link is far more indirect and mediated, although I would not go as far as Scott Soames (and others) and assert that grammatical structure has no role to play in cognition.

In noting that there is a measurable difference in processing effort between 'classical' Hollywood films (as represented in the GS) and the films of the French New Wave, I have shown that a film's structure does partly determine processing complexity. But the descriptions of film structure offered by Metz's structural linguistic–based film semiotics or Colin's cognitive film semiotics based on the Standard Theory of TGG are insufficient in themselves in explaining this processing complexity. This is why I have updated Colin's Standard Theory of film grammar with concepts from Chomsky's trace theory, Sperber and Wilson's principle of relevance, and Jackendoff and Lerdahl's preference rules. Film theory can only benefit from exploring in more detail these and other recent linguistic models.

Conclusion

The compatibility of Chomsky's theory with semiotic views of symbolic function remains to be explored, but will probably find its explanation when both can be integrated into the fabric of a more comprehensive cognitive science. (Thomas Sebeok)[1]

The problem for us is not . . . to complete semiotics, but to transform it. (Michel Colin)[2]

My aim in this book has been to outline the film spectator's cognitive capacity as theorized by the cognitive film semioticians, whose work is united by the same project: to combine film semiotics and cognitive science, with the objective of modelling filmic competence – that is, the spectator's knowledge or intuitions about filmic meaning. To offer an outline of this work I have had to mediate between the insights of the Language Analysis tradition and cognitive science (the twentieth century version of epistemology). As we saw in Chapter 1, these two traditions are usually opposed to one another, since the Language Analysis tradition replaces the epistemologists' assumption that we have immediate access to our own thoughts with the assumption that we only have indirect access to our thoughts via language and other intersubjective sign systems. Chomsky's linguistics creates a synthesis between epistemology and Language Analysis, thus avoiding the idealism and first person perspective of epistemology and the (quasi) behaviorism of the Language Analysis tradition. Chomsky's work on competence therefore epitomizes what this book is all about.

More specifically, the cognitive film semioticians study filmic competence by integrating with film semiotics insights from enunciation theory, pragmatics, as well as Chomsky's transformational generative grammar. To this extent, the cognitive film semioticians are exploring the compatibility of Chomsky's theory with semiotics that Thomas Sebeok calls for. Enunciation theory, pragmatics, and transformational grammar have given the work of the cognitive film semioticians theoretical coherence – explicit, rigorous, precise, and clear aims and objectives. Throughout this book I have used their work as the starting point to study specific and fundamental issues concerning filmic competence, including the spectator's intuitions about filmic space (the construction of a coherent space, the status of off-screen space, intuitions about the frame and diegesis as containers); intuitions about how the film addresses the spectator (different modes of address and spatial orientation); the spectator's different modes of attention required to comprehend different modes of film; and finally, intuitions concerning film sequencing and the comprehension of 'deviant' but acceptable filmic sequences.

But before suggesting that it is possible to develop a complete rapprochement between semiotics and cognitivism, we need to address one final issue – the cognitivists' critique of Grand Theory.

Post-Theory?

The term 'theory' is used in this book to mean 'speculative thought', or thought that goes beyond phenomena to model the non-perceptible reality underlying phenomena. Semiotics is the quintessential speculative theory because, as Thomas Sebeok remarks, "What a semiotic model depicts is not 'reality' as such, but nature as unveiled by our method of questioning."[3] Among the dominant aspects of nature that semiotics and transformational grammar unveil are the scope and limits of human reasoning. The disciplines and authorities that constitute this book's foundations do not, therefore, exclusively study small scale, medium-level issues, but continue to construct universal frameworks. This is why I continue to use the term 'theory' in the singular.

For David Bordwell and Noël Carroll,[4] localized, middle-level (or piecemeal) theories should replace film theory. Moreover, they argue that theorizing should be conceived as an activity (accounting for their use of the present participle 'theorizing') that, finally, should be problem-driven rather than doctrine-driven. There are two immediate responses to this re-configuration of film theory, one serious, the other less serious. First, I am reminded of the story of the elephant and the six blind men. The one who felt the elephant's leg said that it was like a tree trunk; the second, who felt its tail, said it was like a rope; the third, who touched the elephant's trunk, said it was like a hose; and so on. Piecemeal theorizing may not be able to see the wood for the trees if it completely abandons the tendency to develop a unifying theory. My second response suggests that theory and piecemeal theorizing are not incompatible.

The initial stage of the theoretical activity involves the simplification (abstraction and idealization) of the domain under study. For Robert de Beaugrande: "On first inspection, the phenomenal domain is composed of an unruly aggregate of objects and events for which the theorists hope to discover categories, regularities, and principles of order. This step can never be achieved without 'rarefying' and 'abstracting' the phenomena by judging at least some concrete aspects to be irrelevant, accidental, and insignificant."[5] For example, structural linguists propose that only a single description – of the minimum units of linguistic meaning – is necessary to describe the inner logic of natural language's structure. This accounts for Saussure's exclusive emphasis upon *langue* at the expense of *parole*, which he regarded as being too individualistic to come under scientific scrutiny.

This activity of simplifying is the necessary, initial first step in constructing a theory. The early stages of any theory are governed by attempts to obtain the maximum amount of simplicity by studying only the essential determinants of a particular domain. But as research progresses, those determinants deemed inessential and irrelevant at the early stages take on a greater importance and make the research domain complex – in the negative sense that the theory cannot successfully subsume important factors within its framework. For research to progress, this 'negative complexity' must be translated into 'positive complexity' – in other words, the theory must expand to take into account these additional factors.[6]

In attempting to establish itself as a science, structural linguistics followed the simplicity principle and attempted to reduce, by as much as possible, the negative complexity of its research domain, by studying only those characteristics of natural language posited to be linguistically specific. This move toward the study of linguistic specificity resulted in the organization of linguistic data into binary oppositions, which in turn resulted in the development of a segmental methodology to identify these binary oppositions. This approach worked well with the identification of minimal units (distinctive features and phonemes) but reached its saturation point at the level of morphemes.

This process of simplifying eventually and inevitably leads to a crisis, as the 'inessential' phenomena take on importance. Robert de Beaugrande points out that there are two ways of thinking about this crisis. First, the crisis can be understood in terms of Thomas Kuhn's theory of scientific revolutions.[7] For Kuhn, normal science involves the activity of problem solving. A crisis develops when standard puzzles are exhausted and new ones cannot be solved with the existing framework (or paradigm). A scientific revolution, in Kuhn's definition, involves the setting up of a new paradigm with its own puzzles to be solved. The older paradigm is seen to be incompatible with the newer one, and as a result the older one is simply discarded. Second, de Beaugrande understands the crisis in terms of the concepts of negative complexity and positive complexity. For him, "A productive revolution . . . brings about a real major rise in positive complexity, building upon the 'facts' and 'observations' made available by the preceding paradigm and inheriting its achieved positive complexity. 'Unification revolutions' provide the most glowing example of this continuity."[8]

The cognitivists take the Kuhnian approach to the relation between different film theories by suggesting that they (the cognitivists) are 'starting again', rather than building on previous film theories. By contrast, the advantage of cognitive film semiotics is that it involves a productive revolution by building upon the insights of film semiotics (while discarding psychoanalytic film theory). Cognitive film semiotics inaugurates a productive revolution in relation to modern film theory. It recognizes its tendency to oversimplify and attempts to compensate for this oversimplification by adding cognitive theory to its theoretical framework, leading it away from observational adequacy toward descriptive adequacy (and eventually, explanatory adequacy). The cognitivists also recognize modern film theory's tendency to oversimplify, but their reaction has been to debunk its whole approach to theory by replacing it with piecemeal theorizing. I suggest that this is an overreaction, since piecemeal theorizing can be integrated into a general theoretical approach. To recognize and break down general theoretical problems into smaller, piecemeal theoretical problems does not involve a rejection of theory, as Bordwell and Carroll suggest, but represents its next stage of development.

Notes

Chapter One. The Cognitive Turn in Film Theory

1. Janet Bergstrom, "American Feminism and French Film Theory," *Iris*, 10 (1990): 189.
2. Much of the work of these European authors remains untranslated. However, a sample of translations can be found in *The Film Spectator: From Sign to Mind*, ed. Warren Buckland (Amsterdam: Amsterdam University Press, 1995).
3. I use the term 'modern' rather than 'contemporary' because this type of film theory belongs to the discourse of modernity that emerged from the Enlightenment period of European history.
4. The Institute for Cognitive Studies in Film and Video was set up by Joseph Anderson in 1994 in the Department of Theatre and Film at the University of Kansas.

   It is important to note that David Bordwell writes distinguished works in both film theory and film history. He does not, therefore, see film history as a threat to film theory. Rather, he regards them to be complementary approaches to the cinema (as, indeed, would most film scholars). The threat to film theory comes mainly from the study of new objects and from the adoption of the 'new' methodologies enumerated by Janet Bergstrom in the opening quotation.
5. In my anthology *The Film Spectator* I called these European film theorists the 'new film semiologists'. However, the term 'semiology' is now an archaic term, which only refers to the structural linguistic–based work of the sixties. Throughout this book I shall use the label 'film semiotics'. Furthermore, the addition of the word 'cognitive' indicates the equal status these European film theorists accord to cognitive and semiotic mechanisms in filmic comprehension.
6. Peter Lehman, "Politics, Film Theory, and the Academy," *Journal of Film and Video*, 40, 2 (1988): 49; 50.
7. Noël Carroll, *Theorizing the Moving Image* (Cambridge: Cambridge University Press, 1996): 319. See also Carroll's "Prospects for Film Theory: A Personal Assessment," *Post-Theory: Reconstructing Film Studies*, ed. David Bordwell and Noël Carroll (Madison: The University of Wisconsin Press, 1996): 37–68; esp. 56–68.

8. David Bordwell, *Narration in the Fiction Film* (London: Methuen, 1985): xii.

9. Ibid., 23.

10. Christian Metz, *Film Language: A Semiotics of the Cinema*, trans. Michael Taylor (New York: Oxford University Press, 1974): 95.

11. Christian Metz, *Langage et cinéma* (Paris: Larousse, 1971); *Language and Cinema*, trans. Donna-Jean Umiker-Sebeok (The Hague: Mouton, 1974).

12. In the Preface to *Narration in the Fiction Film*, Bordwell writes, "My aim, stated broadly, is to set forth a poetics of narration" (xiii). In the Conclusion, he writes, "None of what I have said is definitive, but this account of narration may encourage the growth of a valuable realm of knowledge: the historical poetics of cinema" (336).

13. John Deely, Brooke Williams, and Felicia E. Kruse, Introduction to *Frontiers in Semiotics* (Bloomington: Indiana University Press, 1986): xi.

14. Boris Glinskij, Boris Grjaznov, Boris Dynin, and Evgenij Nikitin, quoted in P. N. Denisov, *Principles of Constructing Linguistic Models* (The Hague: Mouton, 1973): 154.

15. Metz, *Language and Cinema*, Chapter 10.

16. Ferdinand de Saussure, *Course in General Linguistics*, trans. Roy Harris (London: Duckworth 1983): 8.

17. Samuel Weber, "Saussure and the Apparition of Language: The Critical Perspective," *Modern Language Notes*, 91 (1976): 916.

18. John Deely, Brooke Williams, and Felicia E. Kruse, Introduction to *Frontiers in Semiotics*, xiv.

19. One fundamental difference between the underlying realities is that natural language's system of codes (*la langue*) is of a different logical type from film's system of codes (cinematic language). *La langue* is of a much higher level of organization than cinematic codes – and indeed, of all other semiotic codes.

20. Raymond Bellour made this point in his interview with Janet Bergstrom: "It's obvious that a film can be very different depending on whether it's constructed more or less by scenes or sequences, or by means of alternating syntagmas and episodic sequences." "Alternation, Segmentation, Hypnosis: Interview with Raymond Bellour," *Camera Obscura*, 3/4 (1979): 86.

21. Metz, "On the Notion of Cinematographic Language," *Movies and Methods*, ed. Bill Nichols (Berkeley: University of California Press, 1976): 587. Metz developed the *grande syntagmatique* in Chapter 4 of *Film Language: A Semiotics of the Cinema*, trans. Michael Taylor (New York: Oxford University Press, 1974).

22. In general terms, Metz argued that "the cinema is not a language system, because it contradicts three important characteristics of the linguistic fact: a language is a *system* of *signs* used for *intercommunication*. Now, like all the arts, and because it is itself an art, the cinema is one-way communication." *Film Language*, 75.

   In more specific terms, Metz avoided the temptation to compare the film image to the sentence. He argued that there is no structural similarity between the two, because the sentence, unlike the image, is also analyzable into codes: "The difference [between image and sentence] is that the sentences of verbal language eventually break down into words, whereas in the cinema, they do not: A film may be segmented into large units ('shots'), but these shots are not *reducible* (in Jakobson's sense) into small, basic, and specific units." *Film Language*, 88.

23. Christian Metz, *Essais sur la signification au cinéma* (Paris: Klincksieck, 1968): 51. Michael Taylor translates this phrase as "a non-system language." *Film Language*, 44.
24. Bordwell, *Narration in the Fiction Film*, xiii.
25. Ibid., 29.
26. Ibid.
27. In reviewing the cognitivists' critique of modern film theory, one must at the very least acknowledge Noël Carroll's condemnation of Marxist and psychoanalytic phases of modern film theory in his *Mystifying Movies: Fads and Fallacies in Contemporary Film Theory* (New York: Columbia University Press, 1988). As I have already discussed this book in detail elsewhere, I shall not discuss it here (see Warren Buckland, "Critique of Poor Reason," *Screen*, 30, 4 [1989]: 80–103). However, it may be worthwhile to respond briefly to Carroll's "Cognitivism, Contemporary Film Theory, and Method: A Response to Warren Buckland" (in *Theorizing the Moving Image*, 321–335), his reply to my review. Firstly, Carroll misunderstands my review of his book as an attack on cognitivism. But my primary aim was to investigate the reasoning behind his extreme interpretation of modern film theory, to examine the logic of his claims and the conditions that make such an extreme interpretation possible. I find *Mystifying Movies* a fascinating read because the extremities of its arguments are innovative (a breath of fresh air) and seductive (as a result of their appeal to common sense and to philosophical modes of reasoning such as the reductio ad absurdum). However, the results are frequently misleading (the breath of fresh air becomes a cold, biting wind), as my review attempts to demonstrate.

Secondly, I criticized the alternative cognitive theory Carroll presented in *Mystifying Movies* because it was insufficiently developed and out of place. It seems that the cognitive sections were hurriedly added as an afterthought. Furthermore, my review did not try to defend the aims of modern film theory in the face of Carroll's critique. After all, I stated near the beginning of my review that "contemporary film theory needs to be critically analysed at its foundations. However, I differ with Carroll in stipulating the manner in which this critique should be carried out" ("Critique of Poor Reason," 83). Both Carroll and Edward Small fail to acknowledge this aspect of my review; for example, Edward Small calls it "reactionary" ("Introduction: Cognitivism and Film Theory," *Journal of Dramatic Theory and Criticism*, 6, 2 [1992]: 171). Such dismissive talk simply attempts to close off any attempt to develop a debate between modern film theory and cognitivism, suggesting that the reader should either accept Carroll's arguments or keep quiet. Is Small's attitude to be taken as an exemplary instance of the dialectical reasoning Carroll calls for? The tone of my review simply implies that Carroll's critique of modern film theory is exaggerated. When a new player enters the intellectual marketplace, she establishes her identity by overstating her case (just think of the slogans propounded by the Russian Formalists in their formative period). This is exactly what Carroll aimed for (and achieved) in his review of Stephen Heath's *Questions of Cinema* in 1982 (the review upon which *Mystifying Movies* is based). Carroll wanted to throw the baby out with the bath water without getting wet. My review argued that we need not go quite so far, but agreed that the bath water needed to be changed.

28. Joseph Anderson, *The Reality of Illusion: An Ecological Approach to Cognitive Film Theory* (Carbondale: Southern Illinois University Press, 1996); Gregory Currie, *Image and Mind: Film, Philosophy, and Cognitive Science* (Cambridge: Cambridge University Press, 1995); Ed Tan, *Emotion and the Structure of Narrative Film: Film as an Emotional Machine* (Hillsdale, N.J.: Lawrence Erlbaum, 1996); Torben Grodal, *Moving Pictures: A New Theory of Film Genres, Feelings, and Cognition* (Oxford: Clarendon Press, 1997).

29. Torben Grodal, *Moving Pictures*, 6. I review Grodal's book in *European Journal of Communication*, 13, 4 (1998): 577–581.

30. Karl-Otto Apel, "The Transcendental Conception of Language-Communication and the Idea of First Philosophy," *History of Linguistic Thought and Contemporary Linguistics*, ed. Herman Parret (Berlin: Walter de Gruyter, 1976): 34.

31. Jürgen Habermas, *Postmetaphysical Thinking: Philosophical Essays*, trans. William Mark Hohengarten (Cambridge: Polity Press, 1992): 208.

32. Gilbert Ryle, *The Concept of Mind* (London: Hutchinson, 1949).

33. Apel discusses how C. S. Peirce transformed Kantian epistemology into Language Analysis in "From Kant to Peirce: the Semiotical Transformation of Transcendental Logic," *Towards a Transformation of Philosophy*, trans. Glyn Adey and David Frisby (London: RKP, 1980): 77–92.

34. Speech act theory, founded by J. L. Austin and systematized by John Searle, is one of the dominant areas of research in pragmatics. For Austin, Language Analysis involves explaining the way utterances are embedded in social institutions, and also specifying what actions utterances perform. Language does not simply express ideas that describe existing states of affairs in the world (the view of logical positivism, which Austin is refuting). In addition, speakers use utterances to perform actions – to promise, create obligations, influence the action of others, and establish social relationships. For example, a priest who utters to a couple, "You are now man and wife" isn't simply describing an existing state of affairs in the world; he is creating a new state of affairs – establishing a social relation between a couple – by means of his utterance. Moreover, this utterance performs its function only if spoken by a genuine priest representing the institution of the church.

More generally, speech act theory attempts to establish what types of acts are performed by speakers and under what conditions a particular act is successful. See J. L. Austin, *How to Do Things with Words* (Oxford: Clarendon Press, 1962), and John Searle, *Speech Acts* (Cambridge: Cambridge University Press, 1969).

35. Jürgen Habermas, *The Philosophical Discourse of Modernity*, trans. Frederick Lawrence (Cambridge: Polity Press, 1987): 315.

36. Ibid., 322–323.

37. Thomas Daddesio, *On Minds and Symbols: The Relevance of Cognitive Science for Semiotics* (Berlin: Mouton de Gruyter, 1995): 49–50.

38. Noam Chomsky, "A Review of B. F. Skinner's *Verbal Behavior*," *Language*, 35, 1 (1959): 26–58.

39. David Bordwell, "Contemporary Film Studies and the Vicissitudes of Grand Theory," *Post-Theory: Reconstructing Film Studies*, ed. David Bordwell and Noël Carroll (Madison: The University of Wisconsin Press, 1996): 22.

40. Ibid.

41. Christopher Norris, *The Contest of Faculties: Philosophy and Theory after Deconstruction* (London: Methuen, 1985): 222.

42. *Language and Cinema*, 19.

43. Metz, "The Imaginary Signifier," *Psychoanalysis and Cinema: The Imaginary Signifier*, trans. Ben Brewster et al. (London: Macmillan, 1982): 1–87.

44. Metz, *L'Énonciation impersonnelle ou le site du film* (Paris: Méridiens Klincksieck, 1991).

45. Noam Chomsky, *Knowledge of Language: Its Nature, Origin, and Use* (New York: Praeger, 1986): 24.

46. Noam Chomsky, *Aspects of the Theory of Syntax* (Cambridge, Mass.: MIT Press, 1965).

47. André Martinet, *Elements of General Linguistics*, trans. Elizabeth Palmer (London: Faber and Faber, 1964).

48. Roman Jakobson and Morris Halle, in *Fundamentals of Language*, 2nd ed. (The Hague: Mouton, 1971), then broke down the phoneme into a bundle of distinct features, which were defined in terms of binary oppositions.

Chapter Two. The Body on Screen and in Frame

1. George Lakoff, *Women, Fire, and Dangerous Things: What Categories Reveal about the Mind* (Chicago: University of Chicago Press, 1987): 386.

2. Christian Metz, "Cinema: Language or Language System?" *Film Language: A Semiotics of the Cinema*, trans. Michael Taylor (New York: Oxford University Press, 1974): 31–91.

3. Metz, "Problems of Denotation in the Fiction Film," *Film Language*, 108–146.

4. Stephen Heath, "The Work of Christian Metz," *Screen Reader 2: Cinema and Semiotics* (London: SEFT, 1981): 141.

5. Umberto Eco, "Articulation of the Cinematic Code," *Movies and Methods*, ed. Bill Nichols (Berkeley: University of California Press, 1976): 590–607. For additional semiotic studies of iconicity, see Eco, *A Theory of Semiotics* (Bloomington: Indiana University Press, 1976): 191–217; Søren Kjørup, "Iconic Codes and Pictorial Speech Acts," *Danish Semiotics*, ed. Jørgen Dines Johansen and Morten Nøjgaard (Copenhagen: Munksgaard, 1987): 101–122.

6. These four terms can be represented in Greimas's semiotic square as follows:

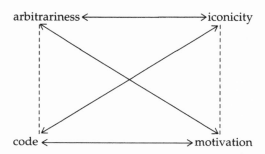

7. Whereas the bottom-up approach to comprehension is empirical, for it emphasizes perceptual input in the perceiver's comprehension process, the top-down approach is cognitive, for it emphasizes the perceiver's cognitive capacity – that is, prior knowledge, expectations, and ability to form hypotheses and make inferences – in the comprehension process.

8. Bordwell, *Narration in the Fiction Film* (London: Methuen, 1985): 49–50.

9. Ibid., 51.

10. Ibid., 33.

11. In relation to this point, Bordwell writes: "It would be an error to take the fabula, or story, as the profilmic event. A film's fabula is never materially present on the screen or soundtrack." Ibid., 49.

12. Lakoff, *Women, Fire, and Dangerous Things*, 116.

13. Bordwell, *Narration in the Fiction Film*, 61–62.

14. Ibid., 62.

15. Ibid.

16. Michel Colin, "Film Semiology as a Cognitive Science," *The Film Spectator: From Sign to Mind*, ed. Warren Buckland (Amsterdam: Amsterdam University Press, 1995): 87–110.

17. Metz, *Language and Cinema*, trans. Donna-Jean Umiker-Sebeok (The Hague: Mouton, 1974): 74.

18. Colin, "Film Semiology as a Cognitive Science," 106.

19. Ibid., 88–89.

20. See Edward Branigan, *Narrative Comprehension and Film* (London: Routledge, 1992): 65.

21. Colin, "Film Semiology as a Cognitive Science," 89.

22. See Umberto Eco, *A Theory of Semiotics*, Chapter 2, esp. 98–114.

23. Dan Sperber and Deirdre Wilson, *Relevance: Communication and Cognition* (Oxford: Basil Blackwell, 1986): 40.

24. Sperber and Wilson, *Relevance*, 43–44.

25. The concept of mutual knowledge has been conceived and developed in the following publications: David Lewis, *Convention* (Cambridge, Mass.: Harvard University Press, 1969): 52–60; Stephen Schiffer, *Meaning* (Oxford: Clarendon Press, 1972): 30–42; and Neil Smith (ed.), *Mutual Knowledge* (London and New York: Academic Press, 1982).

26. Charles M. Eastman, "Representations for Space Planning," *Communication for the Association for Computing Machinery*, 13 (1970): 242–250; Eastman, "Automated Space Planning," *Artificial Intelligence*, 4 (1973): 41–64.

27. Colin, "Film Semiology as a Cognitive Science," 96.

28. Jerry Fodor, *The Modularity of Mind* (Cambridge, Mass.: MIT Press, 1983).

29. Ibid., 36–37.

30. Bordwell, *Narration in the Fiction Film*, 30.

31. Ibid.

32. Colin, "Film Semiology as a Cognitive Science," 104.

33. Ray Jackendoff, *Semantics and Cognition* (Cambridge, Mass.: MIT Press, 1983): 17.

34. Ibid., 16.

35. Bordwell, *Narration in the Fiction Film*, Chapter 2 (discussed in detail in Chapter 1 of this book).

36. Winifred Nöth, "Semiotic Foundations of the Cognitive Paradigm," *Semiosis*, 19, 1 (1994): 5–16.

37. Ibid., 5.

38. Mark Johnson, *The Body in the Mind: The Bodily Basis of Meaning, Imagination, and Reason* (Chicago: University of Chicago Press, 1987); Mark Turner, *Reading Minds: The Study of English in the Age of Cognitive Science* (Princeton, N.J.: Princeton University Press, 1991); Ronald Langacker, *Foundations of Cognitive Grammar*, Volume 1, *Theoretical Prerequisites* (Stanford, Calif.: Stanford University Press, 1987); Volume II, *Descriptive Application* (Stanford, Calif.: Stanford University Press, 1991); Langacker, *Concept, Image, and Symbol: The Cognitive Basis of Grammar* (Berlin: Mouton de Gruyter, 1991); Gilles Fauconnier, *Mental Spaces: Aspects of Meaning Construction in Natural Language* (Cambridge: Cambridge University Press, 1994); Eve Sweester, *Etymology to Pragmatism: Metaphorical and Cultural Aspects of Semantic Structure* (Cambridge: Cambridge University Press, 1990).

39. Lakoff, *Women, Fire, and Dangerous Things*, 266–267. Lakoff's and Johnson's theory of embodied meaning resembles Thomas A. Sebeok's theory of the biosemiotic self. For Sebeok, each species constructs, according to its own unique sensory and bodily structure and functions, its own *Umwelt* (its own perception of the outer world). Because of the variation in the biological makeup of species, it is plausible to argue that different species live in different sensory worlds. See Tho-

mas A. Sebeok, *An Introduction to Semiotics* (London: Pinter Publishers, 1994), esp. 5, 11–12, 113, 122–123.

40. Lakoff, *Women, Fire, and Dangerous Things*, 310.
41. Johnson, *The Body in the Mind*, xvi.
42. Ibid., xxxvii.
43. Ibid., xv.
44. Lakoff, *Women, Fire, and Dangerous Things*, 272–275.
45. Johnson, *The Body in the Mind*, 30–37.
46. Lakoff, *Women, Fire, and Dangerous Things*, 292.
47. Eugene Minkovski, quoted in Sue L. Cataldi, *Emotion, Depth and Flesh: A Study of Sensitive Space – Reflections on Merleau-Ponty's Philosophy of Embodiment* (New York: State University of New York Press, 1993): 50.
48. Crucially for modern film theorists, the process of production is excluded, leaving on screen the finished product. The frame's ability to draw the spectator's attention away from the processes of production is then defined as ideological.
49. Stephen Heath, "On Screen, in Frame: Film and Ideology," *Questions of Cinema* (London: Macmillan, 1981): 13.
50. Heath spells out this opposition between containment and dispersion in the following terms:

    containment – imaginary, signified (positive meaning), stability
    dispersion – symbolic, signifier (negative meaning), flow

    He argues that, in a narrative film, the spectator continually oscillates between containment and dispersion. To explain how this oscillation operates, Heath employs the concept of 'suture', which refers to an interminable process that continually re-positions the spectator in an imaginary relation to the film. This process designates an oscillation between the spectator's gradual recognition of the image as signifier (as part of the symbolic – that is, a lack, or absence) and the replacement of that image with another that temporarily cancels out that lack or absence (thus re-establishing the spectator's imaginary relation to the film). Suture therefore designates a process mediating between the imaginary and the symbolic. Moreover, this oscillation does not simply operate from image to image, but from image to image through the spectator (who poses the lack in one image, motivating the cut to the next): "The major emphasis in all this is that the articulation of the signifying chain of images, of the chain of images as signifying, works not from image to image but from image to image through the absence that the subject constitutes [or poses]." Heath, *Questions of Cinema*, 88.
51. Etienne Souriau, "La structure de l'univers filmique et le vocabulaire de la filmologie," *Revue Internationale de Filmologie*, 7–8 (1951): 231–240. My discussion of Souriau is indebted to Edward Lowry, *The Filmology Movement and Film Study in France* (Ann Arbor, Mich.: UMI Research Press, 1985): 84–86.
52. In a few instances, space can be in frame but off-screen – as when a mirror reflects a space not contained on screen.

53. For the most comprehensive theory to date on the point of view shot, see Edward Branigan, *Point of View in the Cinema: A Theory of Narration and Subjectivity in Classical Film* (Berlin: Mouton, 1984), and *Narrative Comprehension and Film* (London: Routledge, 1992).

54. For the equivocal use of point of view shots in the films of Fritz Lang, see Raymond Bellour, "On Fritz Lang," *Fritz Lang: The Image and the Look*, ed. Stephen Jenkins (London: BFI, 1981): 26–37. I have written about Spielberg's use of equivocal point of view shots in *Raiders of the Lost Ark* in "A Close Encounter with *Raiders of the Lost Ark*," *Contemporary Hollywood Cinema*, ed. Steve Neale and Murray Smith (London: Routledge, 1998), 166–177.

55. In *Film, Language, and Conceptual Structures. Thinking Film in the Age of Cognitivism* (Amsterdam: Academisch Proefschrift, University of Amsterdam, 1995), Jan Simons presents a detailed application of the source–path–goal schema to Dutch political election campaign films.

Chapter Three. Not What Is Seen through the Window but the Window Itself

1. Christian Metz, "The Impersonal Enunciation, or the Site of Film," in Warren Buckland (ed.), *The Film Spectator: From Sign to Mind* (Amsterdam: Amsterdam University Press, 1995): 145–146.

2. Christian Metz, "Mirror Construction in Fellini's *8½*," *Film Language: A Semiotics of the Cinema*, trans. Michael Taylor (New York: Oxford University Press, 1974): 228–234; Metz, "Story/Discourse (A Note on Two Kinds of Voyeurism)," *Psychoanalysis and Cinema: The Imaginary Signifier*, trans. Ben Brewster, Celia Britton, Alfred Guzzetti, and Annwyl Williams (London: Macmillan, 1982): 91–98; Metz, *L'Énonciation impersonnelle ou le site du film* (Paris: Méridiens Klincksieck, 1991). Throughout this chapter, I shall primarily refer to the first section of this book, translated into English as "The Impersonal Enunciation, or the Site of Film," in *The Film Spectator: From Sign to Mind*, 140–163.

3. For a more general overview of Francesco Casetti's work (but one that does not discuss his deictic theory of filmic enunciation in any detail), see Giuliana Muscio and Roberto Zemignan, "Francesco Casetti and Italian Film Semiotics," *Cinema Journal*, 30, 2 (Winter 1991): 23–46.

4. Metz, "The Impersonal Enunciation," 146.

5. Ibid., 159.

6. Ibid.

7. Francesco Casetti, *Dentro lo sguardo: Il filme e il sou spettatore* (Milano: Bompiani, 1986), translated into French as *D'Un regard l'autre: Le film et son spectateur*, trans. Jean Châteauvert and Martine Joly (Lyon: Presses Universitaires de Lyon, 1990); English translation forthcoming from Indiana University Press.

8. Metz, "Sur une traversée des Alpes et des Pyrénées . . . ," Preface to Casetti, *D'Un regard l'autre*, 5–10.

9. See *L'Énonciation impersonnelle*, part II, 37–172, where Metz outlines ten forms of filmic enunciation.
10. Francesco Casetti, "Looking for the Spectator," *Iris*, 2 (1983): 19.
11. Ibid., 21.
12. Ibid., 22.
13. For a more detailed account of what Casetti means by "text," see his "Le texte du film," *Théorie du film*, ed. Jacques Aumont and Jean-Louis Leutrat (Paris: Albatros, 1980): 41–65.
14. Casetti, "Looking for the Spectator," 24.
15. Ibid., 25.
16. See also Casetti, "Pragmatique et théorie du cinéma aujourd'hui," *Hors Cadre*, 10 (1992): 99–109.
17. Casetti, "Looking for the Spectator," 29.
18. Francesco Casetti, "Face to Face," in *The Film Spectator*, 118–139.
19. Ibid., 118.
20. Ibid., 124. Casetti is aware of the empirical implications of this position, since he notes, "This [position] results in hypotheses that one must conform to, traces that indicate the unfolding of the action, and parameters that must be obeyed" (ibid., 126). In particular, this position suggests that only one meaning can be attributed to these textual marks, a premise Metz deconstructs in "The Impersonal Enunciation."
21. "Face to Face," 128.
22. Ibid., 128–129.
23. Ibid., 129.
24. Ibid., 130.
25. Ibid.
26. Ibid., 131.
27. Metz, "The Impersonal Enunciation," 141.
28. Ibid., 149–150.
29. Metz also challenges Casetti's characterization of the film spectator as interlocutor because this term is dependent upon the idea of immediate interaction, which, Metz argues, is absent in film.
30. Metz, "The Impersonal Enunciation," 154.
31. Ibid., 152.
32. Ibid., 153.
33. Ibid., 150.
34. Ibid., 150–151.
35. Ibid., 151.
36. Ibid.
37. Ibid., 154–155.
38. Ibid., 147–148.
39. Ibid., 146.
40. Ibid., 153. Yet, at the same time, Metz does stress that film vaguely acknowledges the extra-textual spectator, both in his revolver example (the 'here is' acknowledges the presence of a spectator), as well as in his later work, particularly "The Imaginary Signifier," where Metz states that film exists *for* the spectator. This is quite evident in the

frontality of the *mise-en-scène*, in camera angles and camera movement, and in the shifts from omniscient to restricted narration, all designed to aid (or deliberately block) the spectator's access to the film's diegesis.

41. We need to remember that Benveniste introduces the distinction between *histoire* and *discours* in order to offer an adequate classification of the various tense forms in modern French, since (and this is the main argument behind Benveniste's paper – see note 42) the traditional grammarian's exclusive reliance upon temporal divisions is insufficient. *Discours* and *histoire* therefore represent two different but complementary planes of utterance, each manifesting a distinct tense system in modern French.

42. Emile Benveniste, "The Correlations of Tense in the French Verb," *Problems in General Linguistics,* trans. Mary Elizabeth Meek (Coral Gables; Fla.: University of Miami Press, 1971): 210.

43. Karl Bühler, quoted in Achim Eschbach, "Editor's Introduction – Karl Bühler: Sematologist," Karl Bühler, *Theory of Language: The Representational Function of Language,* trans. Donald Fraser Goodwin (Amsterdam: John Benjamins, 1990): xxix.

44. Karl Bühler, *Theory of Language,* 145 (emphasis in the original).

45. Daniel Dayan and Elihu Katz, "Electronic Ceremonies: Television Performs a Royal Wedding," *On Signs,* ed. Marshall Blonsky (Baltimore: The Johns Hopkins University Press, 1985): 16–32.

46. Judith Halberstam, *Skin Shows: Gothic Horror and the Technology of Monsters* (Durham, N.C.: Duke University Press, 1995): 167.

47. Ibid., 166–167.

48. David Rodowick, *The Difficulty of Difference: Psychoanalysis, Sexual Difference and Film Theory* (London and New York: Routledge, 1991): 135.

49. Tom Conley, *Film Hieroglyphs: Ruptures in Classical Cinema* (Minneapolis and Oxford: The University of Minnesota Press, 1991): xxxi.

50. Metz, "The Imaginary Signifier," 15, 17, 79, and 80. See also "Story/ Discourse," 92–93.

51. Metz, "The Impersonal Enunciation," 157.

Chapter Four. The Institutional Context

1. Roger Odin, "Approche sémio-pragmatique, approche historique," *Kodikas/Code,* 17, 1–4 (1994): 27–28.

2. Stepehen Levinson, *Pragmatics* (Cambridge: Cambridge University Press, 1983): 32.

3. Bronislaw Malinowski, *A Scientific Theory of Culture and Other Essays* (Chapel Hill: The University of North Carolina Press, 1944): 39.

4. For an outline of these recent debates, see the opening of Noël Carroll's essay, "From Real to Reel: Entangled in Nonfiction Film," *Theorizing the Moving Image* (Cambridge: Cambridge University Press, 1996): 224–252.

5. Francesco Casetti, "Pragmatique et théorie du cinéma aujourd'hui," *Hors Cadre*, 7 (1989): 104.

6. Melina Sinclair, "Fitting Pragmatics in the Mind: Some Issues in Mentalist Pragmatics," *Journal of Pragmatics*, 23 (1995): 509–539.

7. Jan Nuyts, *Aspects of a Cognitive-Pragmatic Theory of Language: On Cognition, Functionalism, and Grammar* (Amsterdam: John Benjamins, 1992); Diane Blakemore, *Understanding Utterances* (Oxford: Basil Blackwell, 1992); Asa Kasher, "On the Psychological Reality of Pragmatics," *Journal of Pragmatics*, 8 (1984): 539–557; Dan Sperber and Deirdre Wilson, *Relevance: Communication and Cognition* (Oxford: Basil Blackwell, 1986).

8. Roger Odin, "La sémio-pragmatique du cinéma sans crise, ni désillusion," *Hors Cadre*, 7 (1989): 83–84.

9. Christian Metz, *Language and Cinema*, trans. Donna-Jean Umiker-Sebeok (The Hague: Mouton, 1974).

10. Ibid., 73–74.

11. Odin, "La sémio-pragmatique du cinéma," 84.

    But Jan Simons is critical of Odin's direct cognitive re-reading of *Language and Cinema* (Jan Simons, "Cognitivism and Pragmatics," unpublished ms., 1991). He begins by agreeing with Odin: "Odin is . . . right when he claims that the description of the codes of a language (e.g. the cinematographic language) has some cognitive relevance, insofar as the 'understanding of film' can be considered as the result of some decoding" (2–3). But he questions Odin's assumption that "the spectator 'decodes' the filmic text in pretty much the same way as the semiologist does (which means with the same cognitive tools and procedures of segmentation and commutation)" (3). Simons is critical of this assumption because "the object of description and explanation of structuralist linguistics is not the knowledge of language-speakers, but the immanent structure of the language system" (5). Finally, he argues that Odin's assumption is too literal because "even the most simple textual analysis of even a very small segment of a film very quickly reaches a degree of complexity a 'natural spectator' is very unlikely to perform in one viewing of a film" (7).

12. Christian Metz, *Psychoanalysis and Cinema: The Imaginary Signifier*, trans. Ben Brewster, Alfred Guzzetti, Celia Britton, and Annwyl Williams (London: Macmillan, 1982).

13. *Language and Cinema*, 121–128.

14. Roy Harris, *Reading Saussure* (London: Duckworth, 1987): 24–25.

15. Ibid., 205.

16. Ibid., 216.

17. Roger Odin, "A Semio-Pragmatic Approach to the Documentary Film," *The Film Spectator: From Sign to Mind*, ed. Warren Buckland (Amsterdam: University of Amsterdam Press, 1995): 227.

18. Sperber and Wilson, *Relevance*, 125.

19. David Bordwell, *Making Meaning: Inference and Rhetoric in the Interpretation of Cinema* (Cambridge, Mass.: Harvard University Press, 1989): 8–9.

20. Ibid.
21. Metz, *Psychoanalysis and Cinema*, 3.
22. Bordwell, *Making Meaning*, 270.
23. Barbara Klinger, *Melodrama and Meaning: History, Culture, and the Films of Douglas Sirk* (Bloomington: Indiana University Press, 1994).
24. Ibid., xv.
25. Ibid.
26. Ibid., xix.
27. Ibid., 127.
28. Odin, "Sémio-pragmatique du cinéma et de l'audiovisuel: Modes et institutions," *Towards a Pragmatics of the Audio-Visual*, Vol. 1, ed. Jürgen Müller (Münster: Nodus Publikationen, 1994): 33–46.
29. Odin, "For a Semio-Pragmatics of Film," *The Film Spectator: From Sign to Mind*, 222.
30. Odin, "Rhétorique du film de famille," *Revue d'Esthétique*, 1–2 (1979): 368.
31. Branigan, "On the Analysis of Interpretive Language, Part I," *Film Criticism*, XVII, 2–3 (1993): 8.
32. Jan Simons, "Pragmatics, Deixis, and the Political Election-Campaign Film," *Towards a Pragmatics of the Audio-Visual*, Vol. 1, 79.
33. Ibid., 82.
34. Roger Odin, "Du spectateur fictionalisant au nouveau spectateur: approche sémio-pragmatique," *Iris*, 8 (1988): 121–139.
35. A. J. Greimas and J. Courtés, *Semiotics and Language: An Analytical Dictionary*, trans. Larry Crist et al. (Bloomington: Indiana University Press, 1982): 119.
36. Umberto Eco, "Articulation of the Cinematic Code," *Movies and Methods*, ed. Bill Nichols (Berkeley: University of California Press, 1976): 590–607.
37. Edward Branigan, "Diegesis and Authorship in Film," *Iris*, 7 (1986): 44.
38. Odin, "Du spectateur fictionnalisant," 124.
39. Ibid.
40. Genette, discussed on page 125 of "Du spectateur fictionalisant."
41. John Searle, "The Logical Status of Fictional Discourse," *Expression and Meaning* (Cambridge: Cambridge University Press, 1979): 60–61.
42. Richard Allen, *Projecting Illusion: Film Spectatorship and the Impression of Reality* (Cambridge: Cambridge University Press, 1995): 135–143.
43. Ibid., 138–139.
44. André Gaudreault, *Du littéraire au filmique: Système du récit* (Paris: Méridiens Klincksieck, 1988), Chapter VIII, and "Narration and Monstration in the Cinema," *Journal of Film and Video*, 39, 2 (1987): 29–36.
45. Roger Odin, "Mise en phase, déphasage et performitivé dans *Le Tempestaire* de Jean Epstein," *Communications* 38 (1983): 213–238.
46. Ibid., 225.
47. "Du spectateur fictionnalisant," 127–128.
48. Ibid., 128.

49. Ibid.
50. Roger Odin, "Sémio-pragmatique du cinéma et de l'audiovisuel: Modes et institutions," *Towards a Pragmatics of the Audio-Visual*, Vol. 1, 33–46.
51. Ibid., 39.
52. Metz, *Psychoanalysis and Cinema*, 7.
53. Odin, "Sémio-pragmatique du cinéma et de l'audiovisuel," 41.
54. Odin, "Approche sémio-pragmatique, approche historique," 28.
55. Odin, "Film documentaire, lecture documentarisante," *Cinémas et réalités*, ed. J. Lyant and Roger Odin (Saint-Etienne: Cierec, 1984): 263–280.
56. Odin, "Film documentaire, lecture documentarisante," 276.
57. Greimas and Courtés, *Semiotics and Language: An Analytical Dictionary*, 307–308.
58. Odin, "Film documentaire, lecture documentarisante," 266.
59. Ibid., 268–269.
60. Ibid., 273.
61. Odin, "Sémio-pragmatique du cinéma et de l'audiovisuel," 34. More recently, Odin has edited a book on the home movie: *Le film de famille*, ed. Roger Odin (Paris: Méridiens Klincksieck, 1995).
62. Odin, "Rhétorique du film de famille," *Revue d'Esthétique*, 1–2 (1979): 240–273.
63. Ibid., 345.
64. Ibid., 348–353.
65. Ibid., 356.
66. Ibid., 366.
67. Odin, "Du spectateur fictionalisant," 132.
68. Odin, *Cinéma et production de sens* (Paris: Editions Armand Colin, 1990): 244.
69. Odin, "Du spectateur fictionalisant," 133.
70. Ibid., 134.
71. Bordwell, *Making Meaning*, 271. Bordwell's theory of parametic narration is developed in Chapter 12 of *Narration in the Fiction Film* (London: Methuen, 1985); his analysis of Ozu's films is to be found in *Ozu and the Poetics of Cinema* (Princeton, N.J.: Princeton University Press, 1988).
72. Bordwell, *Narration in the Fiction Film*, 275–277.
73. Ibid., 274.
74. Richard Allen (personal communication) suggests that it would also be possible to begin thinking of the actant of the documentary film as fictional (the documentary's implied author), a process that would bring fiction and documentary even closer together.
75. Wolfgang Iser, *Prospecting: From Reader Response to Literary Anthropology* (Baltimore: The Johns Hopkins University Press, 1989), and *The Fictive and the Imaginary: Charting Literary Anthropology* (Baltimore: The Johns Hopkins University Press, 1993).
76. Iser, *Prospecting*, 265.
77. Ibid., 267.

Chapter Five. All in the Mind?

1. Noam Chomsky, *Aspects of the Theory of Syntax* (Cambridge, Mass.: MIT Press, 1965): 4.
2. Dominique Chateau, *Le cinéma comme langage* (Brussels: AISS – Publications de la Sorbonne, 1987): 50.
3. David Bordwell, "Contemporary Film Studies and the Vicissitudes of Grand Theory," *Post-Theory: Reconstructing Film Studies*, ed. David Bordwell and Noël Carroll (Madison: The University of Wisconsin Press, 1996): 22.
4. Noam Chomsky, *Current Issues in Linguistic Theory* (The Hague: Mouton, 1964): 8–9.
5. Chomsky, *Aspects*, 24.
6. Chomsky, in Robert Reiber, *Dialogues on the Psychology of Language and Thought* (New York: Plenum Press, 1983): 42.
7. Chomsky, "Linguistics and Adjacent Fields: A Personal View," *The Chomskyan Turn*, ed. Asa Kasher (Oxford: Basil Blackwell, 1991): 9.
8. Scott Soames, "Linguistics and Psychology," *Linguistics and Philosophy*, 7, 2 (1984): 155–179.
9. Ibid., 165.
10. Ibid.
11. Ibid.
12. Michel Colin, "The Grande Syntagmatique Revisited," *The Film Spectator: From Sign to Mind*, ed. Warren Buckland (Amsterdam: Amsterdam University Press, 1995): 45–86.
13. Ibid., 50.
14. Colin, "The Grande Syntagmatique Revisited," 47–48.
15. Christian Metz, *Film Language: A Semiotics of the Cinema*, trans. Michael Taylor (New York: Oxford University Press, 1974): 146.
16. For Metz, on the other hand, the dominant asymmetry in the GS lies within the autonomous shot, which is divided into two heterogeneous sub-types – the sequence shot and four types of insert. The tree diagram of the GS also shows the class of sequence re-written as two syntagmatic types. But Colin finds this acceptable (presumably because it marks the closure of the GS).
17. Metz, *Film Language*, 126.
18. Colin, "The Grande Syntagmatique Revisited," 67.
19. Ibid., 73.
20. Colin distinguishes the scene from the sequence in terms of the way they each represent space. The scene is founded on the unity of what Colin calls a 'spatial frame', whereas the sequence is founded on the unity of an action that may take place across different spaces (the action creates a path, not a spatial frame). Colin indicates this distinction by means of the <inclusive> feature: "This <inclusive> feature means that the scene shows relationships of inclusion between the spaces" (ibid., 74).

21. Ibid.
22. Ibid., 58.
23. Ibid., 75.
24. Metz, "Rapport sur l'état actuel de la sémiologie du cinéma dans le monde (debut 1974)," *A Semiotic Landscape/Panorama Sémiotique*, ed. Seymour Chatman, Umberto Eco, and Jean-Marie Klinkenberg (The Hague: Mouton, 1979): 151.
25. Chateau, *Le cinéma comme langage*, 52.
26. Ibid., 59.
27. Ibid., 58.
28. Noam Chomsky, "Degrees of Grammaticalness," *The Structure of Language: Readings in the Philosophy of Language*, ed. Jerry A. Fodor and Jerrold J. Katz (Englewood Cliff, N.J.: Prentice-Hall, 1964): 387.
29. Jerrold J. Katz, "Semi-Sentences," *The Structure of Language*, ed. Fodor and Katz, 400–416.
30. Ibid., 410–411.
31. Ibid., 411.
32. Chomsky, *Aspects*, 11.
33. Metz, "Modern Cinema and Narrativity," *Film Language*, 185–227.
34. Metz, "Modern Cinema and Narrativity," 211.
35. Ibid.
36. Ibid., 219 (emphasis in the original).
37. Chomsky, "Degrees of Grammaticalness," 384.
38. Noam Chomsky, *Language and the Problems of Knowledge*, 81.
39. Metz, "Modern Cinema and Narrativity," *Film Language*, 219.
40. David Bordwell, *Narration in the Fiction Film* (London: Methuen, 1985): 213–228.
41. Ibid., 217–218.
42. Ibid., 218.
43. Ibid., 211.
44. Ibid., 213.
45. Fred Lerdahl and Ray Jackendoff, *A Generative Theory of Tonal Music*, 9.
46. Ibid., 310. This is, in fact, Lerdahl and Jackendoff's restatement of H. P. Grice's conversational maxim of relation, from which Sperber and Wilson's principle of relevance derives.
47. Metz, *Film Language*, 117.
48. Ibid.
49. Eric Wanner, "Psychology and Linguistics in the Sixties," *The Making of Cognitive Science: Essays in Honour of George A. Miller*, ed. William Hirst (Cambridge: Cambridge University Press, 1988): 144.
50. Colin, "The Grande Syntagmatique Revisited," 80.
51. Ibid., 81.
52. Scott Soames, "Linguistics and Psychology," 162.
53. Thomas G. Bever, "The Psychological Reality of Grammar," *The Making of Cognitive Science: Essays in Honour of George A. Miller*, ed. William Hurst, 132–133.

54. John M. Carroll, "Linguistics, Psychology, and Cinema Theory," *Semiotica* 20, 1–2 (1977): 180.
55. Ibid., 183–184.
56. John M. Carroll, *Toward a Structural Psychology of Cinema* (The Hague: Mouton, 1980).
57. Ibid., 194.
58. Ibid., 69.
59. Carroll, "A Program for Cinema Theory," *Journal of Aesthetics and Art Criticism*, 35 (1977): 344.
60. In the central chapters of his book, Carroll uses TGG in a purely analogous manner, arbitrarily converting filmic events into re-write rules. The cognitive film semioticians discussed in this book do not use linguistics in such an arbitrary and forced manner.
61. Carroll, *Toward a Structural Psychology of the Cinema*, 118.
62. Ibid., 200–203.

Conclusion

1. Thomas Sebeok, *An Introduction to Semiotics* (London: Pinter, 1994): 112.
2. Michel Colin, *Langue, film, discours: prolégomènes à une sémiologie générative du film* (Paris: Klincksieck, 1985): 15.
3. Sebeok, *An Introduction to Semiotics*, 4.
4. David Bordwell and Noël Carroll, eds., *Post-Theory: Reconstructing Film Studies* (Madison: University of Wisconsin Press, 1996).
5. Robert de Beaugrande, "Complexity and Linguistics in the Evolution of Three Paradigms," *Theoretical Linguistics*, 17, 1–3 (1991): 45.
6. Negative complexity characterizes a situation in which the phenomena in the domain under study become too heterogeneous to be theorized. Positive complexity characterizes a situation in which the phenomena in the domain can be theorized successfully.
7. Thomas Kuhn, *The Structure of Scientific Revolutions* (Chicago: University of Chicago Press, 1970).
8. Robert de Beaugrande, "Complexity and Linguistics," 48.

Bibliography of Works Cited

General

Apel, Karl-Otto, "The Transcendental Conception of Language-Communication and the Idea of First Philosophy," *History of Linguistic Thought and Contemporary Linguistics*, ed. Herman Parret (Berlin: Walter de Gruyter, 1976).

"From Kant to Peirce: the Semiotical Transformation of Transcendental Logic," *Towards a Transformation of Philosophy*, trans. Glyn Adey and David Frisby (London: RKP, 1980): 77–92.

Austin, J. L., *How to Do Things with Words* (Oxford: Clarendon Press, 1962).

Benveniste, Emile, "The Correlations of Tense in the French Verb," *Problems in General Linguistics,* trans. Mary Elizabeth Meek (Coral Gables, Fla.: University of Miami Press, 1971): 205–215.

Bever, Thomas G., "The Psychological Reality of Grammar," *The Making of Cognitive Science: Essays in Honour of George A. Miller*, ed. William Hirst (Cambridge: Cambridge University Press, 1988).

Blakemore, Diane, *Understanding Utterances* (Oxford: Basil Blackwell, 1992).

Bühler, Karl, *Theory of Language: The Representational Function of Language*, trans. Donald Fraser Goodwin (Amsterdam: John Benjamins, 1990).

Cataldi, Sue L., *Emotion, Depth and Flesh: A Study of Sensitive Space – Reflections on Merleau-Ponty's Philosophy of Embodiment* (New York: State University of New York Press, 1993).

Chomsky, Noam, "A Review of B. F. Skinner's *Verbal Behavior*," *Language*, 35, 1 (1959): 26–58.

"Degrees of Grammaticalness," *The Structure of Language: Readings in the Philosophy of Language*, ed. Jerry A. Fodor and Jerrold J. Katz (Englewood Cliffs, N.J.: Prentice-Hall, 1964).

Current Issues in Linguistic Theory (The Hague: Mouton, 1964).

Aspects of the Theory of Syntax (Cambridge, Mass.: MIT Press, 1965).

Knowledge of Language: Its Nature, Origin, and Use (New York: Praeger, 1986).

"Linguistics and Adjacent Fields: A Personal View," *The Chomskyan Turn*, ed. Asa Kasher (Oxford: Basil Blackwell, 1991).

Daddesio, Thomas, *On Minds and Symbols: The Relevance of Cognitive Science for Semiotics* (Berlin: Mouton de Gruyter, 1995).

De Beaugrande, Robert, "Complexity and Linguistics in the Evolution of Three Paradigms," *Theoretical Linguistics*, 17, 1–3 (1991): 43–73.

Deely, John, Brooke Williams, and Felicia E. Kruse (eds.), *Frontiers in Semiotics* (Bloomington: Indiana University Press, 1986).

Denisov, P. N., *Principles of Constructing Linguistic Models* (The Hague: Mouton, 1973).

De Saussure, Ferdinand, *Course in General Linguistics*, trans. Roy Harris (London: Duckworth 1983).

Eastman, Charles M., "Representations for Space Planning," *Communication for the Association for Computing Machinery*, 13 (1970): 242–250.

    "Automated Space Planning," *Artificial Intelligence*, 4 (1973): 41–64.

Eco, Umberto, *A Theory of Semiotics* (Bloomington: Indiana University Press, 1976).

Fauconnier, Gilles, *Mental Spaces: Aspects of Meaning Construction in Natural Language* (Cambridge: Cambridge University Press, 1994).

Fodor, Jerry, *The Modularity of Mind* (Cambridge, Mass.: MIT Press, 1983).

Greimas, A. J., and J. Courtés, *Semiotics and Language: An Analytical Dictionary*, trans. Larry Crist et al. (Bloomington: Indiana University Press, 1982).

Habermas, Jürgen, *The Philosophical Discourse of Modernity*, trans. Frederick Lawrence (Cambridge: Polity Press, 1987).

    Postmetaphysical Thinking: Philosophical Essays, trans. William Mark Hohengarten (Cambridge: Polity Press, 1992).

Harris, Roy, *Reading Saussure* (London: Duckworth, 1987).

Iser, Wolfgang, *Prospecting: From Reader Response to Literary Anthropology* (Baltimore: The Johns Hopkins University Press, 1989).

    The Fictive and the Imaginary: Charting Literary Anthropology (Baltimore: The Johns Hopkins University Press, 1993).

Jackendoff, Ray, *Semantics and Cognition* (Cambridge, Mass.: MIT Press, 1983).

Jakobson, Roman, and Morris Halle, *Fundamentals of Language*, 2nd ed. (The Hague: Mouton, 1971).

Johnson, Mark, *The Body in the Mind: The Bodily Basis of Meaning, Imagination, and Reason* (Chicago: University of Chicago Press, 1987).

Kasher, Asa, "On the Psychological Reality of Pragmatics," *Journal of Pragmatics*, 8 (1984): 539–557.

Katz, Jerrold J., "Semi-Sentences," *The Structure of Language: Readings in the Philosophy of Language*, ed. Jerry A. Fodor and Jerrold J. Katz (Englewood Cliffs, N.J.: Prentice-Hall, 1964): 400–416.

Kjørup, Søren, "Iconic Codes and Pictorial Speech Acts," *Danish Semiotics*, ed. Jørgen Dines Johansen and Morten Nøjgaard (Copenhagen; Munksgaard, 1987): 101–122.

Kuhn, Thomas, *The Structure of Scientific Revolutions* (Chicago: University of Chicago Press, 1970).

Lakoff, George, *Women, Fire, and Dangerous Things: What Categories Reveal about the Mind* (Chicago: University of Chicago Press, 1987).

Langacker, Ronald, *Foundations of Cognitive Grammar*, Volume I; *Theoretical*

Prerequisites (Stanford, Calif.: Stanford University Press, 1987); Volume II, *Descriptive Application* (Stanford, Calif.: Stanford University Press, 1991).

Concept, Image, and Symbol: The Cognitive Basis of Grammar (Berlin: Mouton de Gruyter, 1991).

Lerdahl, Fred, and Ray Jackendoff, *A Generative Theory of Tonal Music* (Cambridge, Mass.: MIT Press, 1995).

Levinson, Stephen, *Pragmatics* (Cambridge: Cambridge University Press, 1983).

Lewis, David, *Convention* (Cambridge, Mass.: Harvard University Press, 1969).

Malinowski, Bronislaw, *A Scientific Theory of Culture and Other Essays* (Chapel Hill: The University of North Carolina Press, 1944).

Martinet, André, *Elements of General Linguistics*, trans. Elizabeth Palmer (London: Faber and Faber, 1964).

Norris, Christopher, *The Contest of Faculties: Philosophy and Theory after Deconstruction* (London: Methuen, 1985).

Nöth, Winfried, "Semiotic Foundations of the Cognitive Paradigm," *Semiosis*, 19, 1 (1994): 5–16.

Nuyts, Jan, *Aspects of a Cognitive-Pragmatic Theory of Language: On Cognition, Functionalism, and Grammar* (Amsterdam: John Benjamins, 1992).

Reiber, Robert, *Dialogues on the Psychology of Language and Thought* (New York: Plenum Press, 1983).

Ryle, Gilbert, *The Concept of Mind* (London: Hutchinson, 1949).

Schiffer, Stephen, *Meaning* (Oxford: Clarendon Press, 1972).

Searle, John, *Speech Acts* (Cambridge: Cambridge University Press, 1969).

"The Logical Status of Fictional Discourse," *Expression and Meaning* (Cambridge: Cambridge University Press, 1979): 58–73.

Sebeok, Thomas A., *An Introduction to Semiotics* (London: Pinter Publishers, 1994).

Sinclair, Melina, "Fitting Pragmatics in the Mind: Some Issues in Mentalist Pragmatics," *Journal of Pragmatics*, 23 (1995): 509–539.

Smith, Neil (ed.), *Mutual Knowledge* (London and New York: Academic Press, 1982).

Soames, Scott, "Linguistics and Psychology," *Linguistics and Philosophy*, 7, 2 (1984): 155–179.

Sperber, Dan, and Deirdre Wilson, *Relevance: Communication and Cognition* (Oxford: Basil Blackwell, 1986).

Sweester, Eve, *Etymology to Pragmatism: Metaphorical and Cultural Aspects of Semantic Structure* (Cambridge: Cambridge University Press, 1990).

Turner, Mark, *Reading Minds: The Study of English in the Age of Cognitive Science* (Princeton, N.J.: Princeton University Press, 1991).

Wanner, Eric, "Psychology and Linguistics in the Sixties," *The Making of Cognitive Science: Essays in Honour of George A. Miller*, ed. William Hirst (Cambridge: Cambridge University Press, 1988).

Weber, Samuel, "Saussure and the Apparition of Language: The Critical Perspective," *Modern Language Notes*, 91 (1976).

Film Studies

Allen, Richard, *Projecting Illusion: Film Spectatorship and the Impression of Reality* (Cambridge: Cambridge University Press, 1995).

Anderson, Joseph, *The Reality of Illusion: An Ecological Approach to Cognitive Film Theory* (Carbondale: Southern Illinois University Press, 1996).

Bellour, Raymond, "On Fritz Lang," *Fritz Lang: The Image and the Look*, ed. Stephen Jenkins (London: BFI, 1981): 26–37.

Bergstrom, Janet, "Alternation, Segmentation, Hypnosis: Interview with Raymond Bellour," *Camera Obscura*, 3/4 (1979): 71–103.

"American Feminism and French Film Theory," *Iris*, 10 (1990): 183–197.

Bordwell, David, *Narration in the Fiction Film* (London: Methuen, 1985).

Ozu and the Poetics of Cinema (Princeton, N.J.: Princeton University Press, 1988).

Making Meaning: Inference and Rhetoric in the Interpretation of Cinema (Cambridge, Mass.: Harvard University Press, 1989).

"Contemporary Film Studies and the Vicissitudes of Grand Theory," *Post-Theory: Reconstructing Film Studies*, ed. David Bordwell and Noël Carroll (Madison: The University of Wisconsin Press, 1996): 3–36.

Bordwell, David, and Noël Carroll, eds., *Post-Theory: Reconstructing Film Studies* (Madison: University of Wisconsin Press, 1996).

Branigan, Edward, *Point of View in the Cinema: A Theory of Narration and Subjectivity in Classical Film* (Berlin: Mouton, 1984).

"Diegesis and Authorship in Film," *Iris*, 7 (1986): 37–54.

Narrative Comprehension and Film (London: Routledge, 1992).

"On the Analysis of Interpretive Language, Part I," *Film Criticism*, XVII, 2–3 (1993).

Buckland, Warren, "Critique of Poor Reason," *Screen*, 30, 4 (1989): 80–103.

(ed.), *The Film Spectator: From Sign to Mind* (Amsterdam: Amsterdam University Press, 1995).

"A Close Encounter with *Raiders of the Lost Ark*," *Contemporary Hollywood Cinema*, ed. Steve Neale and Murray Smith (London: Routledge, 1998): 166–177.

review of Torben Grodal, *Moving Pictures*, *European Journal of Communication*, 13, 4 (1998): 577–581.

Carroll, John M., "Linguistics, Psychology, and Cinema Theory," *Semiotica* 20, 1–2 (1977): 173–195.

"A Program for Cinema Theory," *Journal of Aesthetics and Art Criticism*, 35 (1977): 337–351.

Toward a Structural Psychology of Cinema (The Hague: Mouton, 1980).

Carroll, Noël, *Mystifying Movies: Fads and Fallacies in Contemporary Film Theory* (New York: Columbia University Press, 1988).

Theorizing the Moving Image (Cambridge: Cambridge University Press, 1996).

"Cognitivism, Contemporary Film Theory, and Method: A Response to Warren Buckland," *Theorizing the Moving Image* (Cambridge: Cambridge University Press, 1996): 321–335.

"Prospects for Film Theory: A Personal Assessment," *Post-Theory: Reconstructing Film Studies,* ed. David Bordwell and Noël Carroll (Madison: University of Wisconsin Press, 1996): 37–68.

Casetti, Francesco, "Le texte du film," *Théorie du film,* ed. Jacques Aumont and Jean-Louis Leutrat (Paris: Albatros, 1980): 41–65.

"Looking for the Spectator,"*Iris,* 2 (1983): 15–29.

"Pragmatique et théorie du cinéma aujourd'hui," *Hors Cadre,* 7 (1989): 99–109.

D'Un regard l'autre. Le film et son spectateur, trans. Jean Châteauvert and Martine Joly (Lyon: Presses Universitaires de Lyon, 1990).

"Pragmatique et théorie du cinéma aujourd'hui," *Hors Cadre,* 10 (1992): 99–109.

"Face to Face," *The Film Spectator: From Sign to Mind,* ed. Warren Buckland (Amsterdam: Amsterdam University Press, 1995): 118–139.

Chateau, Dominique, *Le cinéma comme langage* (Brussels: AISS – Publications de la Sorbonne, 1987).

Colin, Michel, *Langue, film, discours: prolégomènes à une sémiologie générative du film* (Paris: Klincksieck, 1985).

"The Grande Syntagmatique Revisited," *The Film Spectator: From Sign to Mind,* ed. Warren Buckland (Amsterdam: Amsterdam University Press, 1995): 45–86.

"Film Semiology as a Cognitive Science," *The Film Spectator: From Sign to Mind,* ed. Warren Buckland (Amsterdam: Amsterdam University Press, 1995): 87–110.

Conley, Tom, *Film Hieroglyphs: Ruptures in Classical Cinema* (Minneapolis and Oxford: The University of Minnesota Press, 1991).

Currie, Gregory, *Image and Mind: Film, Philosophy, and Cognitive Science* (Cambridge: Cambridge University Press, 1995).

Dayan, Daniel, and Elihu Katz, "Electronic Ceremonies: Television Performs a Royal Wedding," *On Signs,* ed. Marshall Blonsky (Baltimore: The Johns Hopkins University Press, 1985): 16–32.

Eco, Umberto, "Articulation of the Cinematic Code," *Movies and Methods,* ed. Bill Nichols (Berkeley: University of California Press, 1976): 590–607.

Gaudreault, André, "Narration and Monstration in the Cinema," *Journal of Film and Video,* 39, 2 (1987): 29–36.

Du littéraire au filmique: Système du récit (Paris: Méridiens Klincksieck, 1988).

Grodal, Torben, *Moving Pictures: A New Theory of Film Genres, Feelings, and Cognition* (Oxford: Clarendon Press, 1997).

Halberstam, Judith, *Skin Shows: Gothic Horror and the Technology of Monsters* (Durham, N.C.: Duke University Press, 1995).

Heath, Stephen, "The Work of Christian Metz," *Screen Reader, 2, Cinema and Semiotics* (London: SEFT, 1981): 138–161.

Questions of Cinema (London: Macmillan, 1981).

Klinger, Barbara, *Melodrama and Meaning: History, Culture, and the Films of Douglas Sirk* (Bloomington: Indiana University Press, 1994).

Lehman, Peter, "Politics, Film Theory, and the Academy," *Journal of Film and Video*, 40, 2 (1988).

Lowry, Edward, *The Filmology Movement and Film Study in France* (Ann Arbor, Mich.: UMI Research Press, 1985).

Metz, Christian, *Essais sur la signification au cinéma* (Paris: Klincksieck, 1968).

Film Language: A Semiotics of the Cinema, trans. Michael Taylor (New York: Oxford University Press, 1974).

"Problems of Denotation in the Fiction Film," *Film Language: A Semiotics of the Cinema*, trans. Michael Taylor (New York: Oxford University Press, 1974): 108–146.

Language and Cinema, trans. Donna-Jean Umiker-Sebeok (The Hague: Mouton, 1974).

"On the Notion of Cinematographic Language," *Movies and Methods*, ed. Bill Nichols (Berkeley: University of California Press, 1976): 582–589.

"Rapport sur l'état actuel de la sémiologie du cinéma dans le monde (debut 1974),"*A Semiotic Landscape/Panorama Sémiotique*, ed. Seymour Chatman, Umberto Eco, and Jean-Marie Klinkenberg (The Hague: Mouton, 1979).

"The Imaginary Signifier," *Psychoanalysis and Cinema: The Imaginary Signifier*, trans. Ben Brewster et al. (London: Macmillan, 1982): 1–87.

"Story/Discourse (A Note on Two Kinds of Voyeurism)," *Psychoanalysis and Cinema: The Imaginary Signifier*, trans. Ben Brewster et al. (London: Macmillan, 1982): 91–98.

"Sur une traversée des Alpes Pyrénées . . . ," Preface to Casetti, *D'Un regard l'autre: Le film et son spectateur* (Lyon: Presses Universitaires de Lyon, 1990): 5–10.

L'Énonciation impersonnelle ou le site du film (Paris: Méridiens Klincksieck, 1991).

"The Impersonal Enunciation, or the Site of Film," *in The Film Spectator: From Sign to Mind* (Amsterdam: Amsterdam University Press, 1995): 140–163.

Muscio, Giuliana, and Roberto Zemignan, "Francesco Casetti and Italian Film Semiotics," *Cinema Journal*, 30, 2 (Winter 1991): 23–46.

Odin, Roger, "Rhétorique du film de famille," *Revue d'Esthétique*, 1–2 (1979): 340–373.

"Mise en phase, déphasage et performitivé dans *Le Tempestaire* de Jean Epstein," *Communications* 38 (1983): 213–238.

"Film documentaire, lecture documentarisante," *Cinémas et réalités*, ed. J. Lyant and Roger Odin (Saint-Etienne: Cierec, 1984): 263–280.

"Du spectateur fictionalisant au nouveau spectateur: approche sémio-pragmatique," *Iris*, 8 (1998): 121–139.

"La sémio-pragmatique du cinéma sans crise, ni désillusion," *Hors Cadre*, 7 (1989): 77–92.

Cinéma et production de sens (Paris: Editions Armand Colin, 1990).

"Sémio-pragmatique du cinéma et de l'audiovisuel: Modes et institutions," *Towards a Pragmatics of the Audio-Visual*, Vol. 1, ed. Jürgen Müller (Münster: Nodus Publikationen, 1994): 33–46.

"Approche sémio-pragmatique, approche historique," *Kodikas/Code*, 17, 1–4 (1994): 27–36.

"For a Semio-Pragmatics of Film," *The Film Spectator: From Sign to Mind*, ed. Warren Buckland (Amsterdam: Amsterdam University Press, 1995): 213–226.

"A Semio-Pragmatic Approach to the Documentary Film," *The Film Spectator: From Sign to Mind*, ed. Warren Buckland (Amsterdam: Amsterdam University Press, 1995): 227–235.

(ed.), *Le film de famille* (Paris: Méridiens Klincksieck, 1995).

Rodowick, David, *The Difficulty of Difference: Psychoanalysis, Sexual Difference and Film Theory* (London and New York: Routledge, 1991).

Simons, Jan, "Cognitivism and Pragmatics," unpublished ms., 1991.

"Pragmatics, Deixis, and the Political Election-Campaign Film," *Towards a Pragmatics of the Audio-Visual*, Vol. 1, ed. Jürgen Müller (Münster: Nodus Publikationen, 1994): 77–92.

Film, Language, and Conceptual Structures. Thinking Film in the Age of Cognitivism (Amsterdam: Academisch Proefschrift, University of Amsterdam, 1995).

Small, Edward, "Introduction: Cognitivism and Film Theory," *Journal of Dramatic Theory and Criticism*, 6, 2 (1992): 165–172.

Souriau, Etienne, "La structure de l'univers filmique et le vocabulaire de la filmologie," *Revue Internationale de Filmologie*, 7–8 (1951): 231–240.

Tan, Ed, *Emotion and the Structure of Narrative Film: Film as an Emotional Machine* (Hillsdale, N.J.: Lawrence Erlbaum, 1996).

Index

Printed in Great Britain
by Amazon.co.uk, Ltd.,
Marston Gate.